The Two Roads of Life
Navigating Yourself and Family to Health and Contentment

By Michael J. Simon, PhD
A Retrospective of His Psychology Practice:
Concepts and Interventions for Children and Adults

Edited by Krista Hill of L Talbott Editorial
and Lori Haggard

Designed by Paul J. Hoffman

PathBinder
Publishing
COLUMBUS, INDIANA

Published by PathBinder Publishing
P.O. Box 2611
Columbus, IN 47202
www.PathBinderPublishing.com

Copyright © 2021 by Michael J. Simon
All rights reserved

Front and back covers designed by Anna Perlich

First published in 2021

Manufactured in the United States

ISBN: 978-1-7359962-7-1

Library of Congress Control Number: 2021901034

Note: The information in this book is true and complete to the best of our knowledge. It is offered without guarantee on the part of the author or PathBinder Publishing. The author and PathBinder Publishing disclaim all liability in connection with the use of this book.

All rights reserved. No part of this book may be reproduced or transmitted in any form whatsoever without prior written permission from the publisher except in the case of brief quotations embodied in critical articles and reviews.

On the Experience Road, our lives connect with so many souls. To all of those whom I treated, you were my inspiration for growth, both professionally and personally. It was my honor to have shared these moments with you.

I further dedicate this book to my son, Scott. He provided a relentless source of encouragement. He reminded me to strive high and to live up to that which I had taught him. If you make a reasonably good effort, one can usually expect a reasonably good outcome.

A special thank you to my wife, Maria, whose technological assistance was invaluable, as well as for her shining belief in my effort.

Foreword

I have known Dr. Simon as a colleague and friend for many years.

As a colleague, Mike and I have been members of the same peer supervisory group and, as a result, I have had the pleasure of listening as he described many of the cases he was treating. What I found most striking about these presentations was the depth of understanding they reflected about the human condition and the types of emotional difficulties that can arise.

It has always been my feeling that Mike's insight into behavior transcended knowledge of one therapeutic orientation or another. His case reports more reflected a way of "knowing about people" and how personal experiences can combine with background to result in positive or negative behavior patterns. As Mike spoke about his patients, it was clear that his understanding of their problems was complemented by great compassion for their suffering and an enormous gift for designing effective treatment plans, driven by his understanding and empathy, to help his clients overcome their emotional worries and blocks.

It has been rare, in my experience, to encounter a clinician with the type of broad skillset that Mike evidences. It is even rarer to find someone whose abilities not only allow him to tackle the problems of adults, but also enables him to relate to patients across the developmental spectrum. Yet Mike often presents cases of both children and adults in a way that suggest he is one of few practitioners capable of working in both worlds and of understanding how issues at one stage of life can influence emotional function later on.

In addition to his capacity as a therapist, Mike has proven to be unusually skilled in his ability to help his fellow clinicians understand some of their own complex cases. With great sensitivity and ability to drill down to the core, Mike brings to bear the traits embodied by incisive intellect, concrete life experience, and broad theoretical orientation to bring clarity and direction to highly problematic clinical situations. I have felt especially lucky to have Mike's insight available to me as I worked through problems with the most difficult of my patients.

It has been my great good fortune to have known Mike over these years. He is a warm and caring person and therapist who has dedicated his career to helping people in emotional distress. I have great confidence in Mike's skills and heartily recommend him to those seeking understanding and relief from emotional pain.

— Phil Stein, PhD, Psychologist

Preface

After receiving my doctorate from Hofstra University in 1976, I practiced clinical psychology in suburban Long Island, N.Y., for forty-three years. In 2018, I decided it was time to retire. My wife, Maria, and I relocated to Washington, D.C. for a taste of urban life.

Upon arriving in my new city, I quickly jumped into developing and expanding my interests in natural and environmental sciences. As I began to focus on my new interests, I became aware that I was spending so little of my current time staying conscious of the many methods and treatment schemes I had used in my work. This contrasted with the years of almost daily discussions and involvement with clinical psychology. I became aware, and was truly afraid, that over time I might not be able to recall my experiences. I had devoted a lifetime to acquiring a knowledge base that I feared would fade away. I decided that there needed to be at least a record of what I had accomplished and experienced over so many years of study and clinical interaction. This book is a window into how I applied that knowledge to help others.

Spending years studying and helping people, a clinician will often develop their own unique perspectives. This process is a continuous, developing, ever-changing effort and requires being open to observing, processing, and incorporating new knowledge. Each new interaction modifies one's perspectives. Over the years, I transformed from a hardcore behaviorist into a clinician with an eclectic treatment perspective. My goal was to find that unique set of variables I could use to the benefit of my clients.

I am immensely proud of the innovations I developed to help my clients. I treated children, teens, and adults, families, groups, and individuals. My approach to my practice was based on practical application. I developed and employed, as I viewed it, **a teaching model to treatment**. I found that a vast majority of my clients would become disinterested with complicated psychological jargon. I adhered to the concept of "keep it simple." They needed specific, practical, and easy-to-understand advice.

My focus was on teaching cognitive and behavioral skills, ways of thinking, and new behaviors. My work was also based on understanding the biological aspects of my clients, the systems they lived in, and the philosophies they used to guide their lives. I leaned heavily on my behavioral background but also became very integrative in my treatment approaches, using ego psychology, systems theory, neuro-biological concepts, cognitive constructs, as well as hypnosis.

Over the course of forty-three years, I believe I became highly creative with my methods. My clients seemed to respond well to my teaching approach. My approach was not based on passive listening; I found that I often talked as much during sessions as they did. Although it was necessary to be empathetic and supportive, especially in the initial stages, I found myself eager to move on to problem solving rather than passive supportive approaches. While it was necessary to explore origins of problems, rather than just uncover them, I wanted to script the ideas, philosophies, and habits they had acquired in their lives. In timely moments, as part of my teaching approach, I would share my own life experiences that had shaped my viewpoints. I also shared tales about my hobbies and interests to encourage clients to model and develop their own coping/relaxing activities.

I loved my work and thoroughly enjoyed the challenges my clients presented. I preferred working in private practice rather than for an agency or school. I had a large practice, seeing in total — from groups and individual sessions — about sixty to seventy clients per week. My practice was situated in an area where most of my clients relied on insurance plans to be able to obtain therapy. Each company required a massive amount of paperwork and processing to file claims. I would have liked to have had a smaller practice, but to make a living in private practice, a larger one was necessary to meet the demands of the insurance companies. I eventually had to hire a billing service and a bookkeeper.

Years passed and I plugged away at my practice. Later, I became exhausted from the non-therapeutic demands of the practice, e.g. paperwork, audits, and billing, and I found myself cutting back weekends and, eventually, to four days a week to have time to decompress. My daily schedule over the last few years was 9 a.m. to 7:30 p.m., Monday through Thursday, with thirty minutes for lunch and dinner.

One of the most rewarding aspects of my work involved the monthly peer groups that I attended throughout my career. My colleagues were a pillar of emotional support and an amazing venue in which to learn from others as well as discuss creative methods of treatment. They became my extended family. We laughed, cried, and mourned together. I deeply miss them.

Throughout my years in clinical practice, I had to deal with the same normal stresses we all face, such as raising kids, spousal relationship needs, and keeping a positive sense of self. Life went well for the most part but not without the difficult, critical choices we all face. At times, when facing major, life–altering decisions, I went into my own therapy. I practiced what I preached, becoming a role model for my clients facing similar problems.

When Maria and I began to see retirement on the horizon, we decided to take charge of this transition while we had the health and means to take a break and redirect our future. We are now enjoying our first years of retirement and have been invigorated by the change. I have discovered that retirement is a time to seek out new directions and to reflect on past accomplishments. Currently, I have no plans to return to practice, yet the door is open. There have been so many lessons learned from my years of experience. I, therefore, want to try to record what I developed and not lose this knowledge, perhaps to pass it on to others.

My focus begins with an understanding of the **Experience Road**. Following, I will continue with my family and child model of treatment, **the Family as a Country**. This is an integrative model designed to determine the factors in play when treating a child. This perspective allows for treating the parental needs, the needs of the child, and the systems that bind a family together.

I will branch off to discuss additional treatment approaches for both children and adults. I have worked on issues for special-needs children such as autism, attention-deficit/hyperactivity disorder (ADHD), oppositional defiant disorder (ODD), obsessive-compulsive disorder (OCD), divorce and mourning, and educational problems. With adults, my work focused on relationship problems, communication skills, post-traumatic stress disorder (PTSD), anger management, OCD, depression, and anxiety.

I found I had so much to relate that I decided to break my memories into two volumes, separating children and adults. Even with this separation there is considerable overlap. I encourage the reader to read both volumes. More information regarding my work is also available on my website at **www.DrMichaelJSimonPsychologist.com** and on my blog at Drmjsimon51.medium.com.

— Michael J. Simon

Introduction

While driving in my car several years ago, I happened to listen to an NPR interview with the noted television producer, Norman Lear. Lear was famous for hit comedy shows such as *All in the Family* (Sagal, 2016). The broadcast highlighted his professional longevity (Lear is currently ninety-seven). As I listened, I was astounded by how sharp and quick his mind was. The interviewer highlighted Lear's incredible mental lucidity.

Lear was asked to explain how he maintained his insightful and personable nature. He replied with two words: **Over/Next**. The ensuing discussion focused on the meaning of these two words. As he explained, Lear tried to accept the idea that, when an event passed, it was **over** — let it go. There was no need to obsess or needlessly linger over what was out of his control. He could not change the past, only take what he learned from the event and go on with life. He would then focus his attention to what came **next** in life. With a clearer, less emotionally-burdened mind, he would be open to new life experiences.

Lear's point of view was the essence of what I had been teaching with **Experience Road** thinking. I used this concept of **Over/Next** as a buzz word to teach people to quickly shift back to Experience Road thinking rather than linger unnecessarily on **Failure Road** thinking.

Although I believe in the originality of how I presented my therapeutic concepts, I do not lay claim to them being original ideas. At best, I reinvented how I presented my messages, but the messages have been around throughout the ages. Still, every now and then, hearing my messages being expressed from an unexpected source, such as Norman Lear, reaffirmed credibility and validity for these concepts.

What is the Experience Road?

A life's journey is a path of infinite experiences. At each point along the journey, we receive vast amounts of knowledge. No matter the emotion of that moment, we gain invaluable lessons that can be used to shape and grow our destinies. I call this journey the **Experience Road** of life.

In 1973, I began a journey to develop my skills as a clinical psychologist. Over many years of clinical experiences, I learned valuable lessons that I used to develop and refine my treatment protocols. My journey is reflected in two concepts I am writing about: practice and philosophy.

The Experience Road has been the culmination of this journey. It is an encouraging and helpful guiding philosophy to life — a philosophy that guides my life, and a viewpoint I live by and tried to teach all of my clients. Every event or experience has a lesson to learn. These lessons form how we think and help to develop beliefs that affect and influence how we adjust and grow from life's daily interactions. The Experience Road perspective encourages learning from these lessons, focusing on positive growth rather than obsessing on negative, non-productive outcomes, thus rejecting the concept of failure. If even one thing is learned from any event, it is a success. Therefore, we only succeed — we never fail. This is the essence of the Experience Road. I will be addressing this concept throughout this book.

My teaching approach to treatment is centered on a **mind-body** transformation. How the mind interprets events sets the stage for the body's reaction. It is important to address both aspects when treating behavioral/psychological issues. I usually began first with the mind. My goal was to teach people how our minds work. Understanding this process can make it easier to accept changing our minds, and then our behaviors.

When we are born, we come into the world with a biological foundation but without instructions as to how the world works. At an early age, we are taught how to think by parents, religion, government, social media, and the entertainment world. My goal was to teach and emphasize a philosophy to life that would improve our feelings/reactions by changing how we interpret events.

We have a **choice** in how to think about the world around us. I emphasized throughout my work that there are two roads of life we can travel. I encouraged those I counseled to travel the **Experience Road,** not the **Failure Road.** Everyone I worked with, from child to adult, parent or couple, was taught to try to look at life as a place for learning experiences. As I pointed out, I do not believe in failure. Every moment in life is a learning experience. If you can learn something from an experience, then it is a success and is positive. The key is choosing not to accept failure or negative thinking.

Confronting life's difficulties involves a need to change our programming or philosophy of life. What we believe affects how we interpret sensory input, the actions we choose, and the feelings we experience. The change involves understanding the contrast between the **Experience Road** and the **Failure Road** way of thinking.

People who follow the **Experience Road** of life usually feel happier and more fulfilled. These people accept that failure does not exist. They see every moment as an experience they can learn from. Again, if they learn anything, then it is a success. On this road they are always succeeding; failure does not exist.

Experience Road thinkers tend to live in the here and now. They have learned not to dwell on the past. They also try not to get too far ahead of themselves and over-focus on the future. They can look forward but know that present events will have a greater impact on the unwritten future. Consider the example of taking a test and doing poorly. Someone on the Experience Road takes a step back and thinks, "Ok, it's not horrible, awful, and terrible (**HAT**). It's only frustrating, annoying, and disappointing (**FAD**). I am still alive. Let me see what I can learn from the experience." Then their thinking might be, "Could I have studied differently? Or, could I have organized my notes better? Could I have asked more questions in class or have asked for extra help? Maybe I could have created a study group. Now that I understand what I missed, I can go back and review the material." They might think that, perhaps, the subject is not well suited for them. "I'll take other classes to find out what else I might enjoy instead."

Experience Road travelers pick themselves up and seek out facts. They think **brilliantly** about the situation. They do not put themselves down, and they maintain a positive attitude. They even accept death as a natural condition in life. It will happen to us all. They try to make the best of their lives while they still have some control and choices. On this road, they live in the present without being overly focused on the future. The past is done and gone, but one lives on to explore life and all it can be. The Experience Road approach to thinking is the light they take with them into the unknown. It is only in the unknown, with risks, where new possibilities exist. Doing the same, non-productive things repeatedly is a waste of time, energy, and life.

Take some risks and find new possibilities!

People on this path often have more self-esteem and self-confidence. Not subscribing to the terror of failure, they spend more effort focusing on and trusting in their abilities. People on the Experience Road believe in the concept that:

If you make a reasonably good effort,
you should usually expect a reasonably good result!

Conversely, people who follow the **Failure Road** often experience more disappointment and emotional issues. When something goes wrong on the Failure Road, people put the HAT on and start demanding, catastrophizing, and blaming. When this person takes a test and does poorly, Failure Road thinking means they get all caught up with negative emotions. "This is a stupid test! It should not be so hard! He is a stupid teacher! They think I am stupid!" or maybe, "I am so stupid!" They usually quit and withdraw angrily, or get depressed. Staying on this road over a lifetime will lead to a poor self-image, an unhappy life, and a history of under-achievement, anxiety, and depression. Parenting from a Failure Road perspective is excessively focused on punishment and criticism.

People on the Failure Road often expect the worst-case scenarios to happen. They are afraid to take risks because of what could happen. They live afraid of change. They believe that, if something goes wrong, they will die! People do not like to admit that and often hide it with humor. We hear this jokingly all the time in phrases like, "Oh, I would die of embarrassment," or "I will just dig a hole and bury myself," or "I will jump off a bridge if they reject me."

People on the Failure Road are usually very afraid of the unknown. It is like being afraid of the dark. "I cannot see where I am going. I cannot risk getting hurt or dying. I better not take a risk." Our fear of the dark and death stems from a primitive instinct that goes back to our caveman ancestors. People tend to feel most comfortable when they can see the path. We are diurnal, not nocturnal, creatures.

When our caveman ancestors did not have fire, they huddled in a cave at night with a rock wall to protect them from what was lurking in the dark outside. Then, as they learned to make fire, they sat around the campfire but did not go beyond the fire circle where there could be danger. Over time, they created lanterns and built fortress walls around the towns. With a lantern, they would walk up to the gate but not go beyond the gate where danger and death waited. In the age of electricity, we have strung up lights everywhere. Now we can drive long distances at night with our headlights and streetlamps. However, turn down a dark street with no lights and suddenly we feel frightened!

This is how people on the Failure Road view life. Only go where you can see. Taking a risk is to risk dying. Christopher Columbus once said he wanted to see what was out there beyond the horizon. Some warned he would fall off the edge of the earth. As he set out and people saw his ships fall below the horizon, they said, "There he goes. Columbus is dead. We tried to tell him, but he was too stubborn to listen."

Failure is a negative concept we get programmed with. Get rid of it!

Table of Contents

Foreword	v
Preface	vii
Introduction	xi

Volume One: Childhood Issues and Interventions

The Family as a Country Model	19
Figure 1: Family as a Country	
The Government: Needs of the Parents	21
Figure 2: Parenting Tools	
The Citizens: Needs of the Children	26
Stage One: The Age of Discovery Child	26
Social Behavior of the Age of Discovery Child	30
Discipline with the Age of Discovery Child	31
The Power of Positive Reinforcement with the Age of Discovery Child	36
Restraint Techniques for Aggressive Behavior with the Age of Discovery Child	37
Stage Two: The Age of Opinion Child	41
The System of Law and Order: The "Choose to Earn Privileges" Discipline Model	44
Figure 3: Choose to Earn	45
Active Listening and Problem Solving	49
Teaching Skills to Earn Privileges: Structure	51
Figure 4: Daily Checklist	52
Homework and Study	53
Figure 5: Backpack Checklist	54
Stage Three: Teenage Thinkers	55
The System of Love and Attention	58
Monitoring the Country (Family)	59
Childhood Therapeutic Interventions	60
The Experience Road vs. the Failure Road	61

Cognitive Training	62
Figure 6: Monster Thoughts; Better Thoughts	64
Anger and Frustration Control: A Four-Step Program	65
Figure 7: Anger Frustration Control	66
How to Manage Teasing	67
Assertion and Positive Training	70
Treating Anxiety: Phobias and OCD	74
Toileting Issues	80
Sleep Problems	81
Social-skills Group Therapy for Children	84
Issues of Loss: Divorce and Death	88
Perspectives on ADHD	90

Volume Two: Adults

Introduction	93
How Do You Make a Feeling?	94
The Thinking Brain	96
How Does the Brain Work?	97
Computers and the Brain	99
Demanding, Catastrophizing, and Blaming (DCB)	103
CPA: Child, Parent, and Adult	104
The Attack of the Killer ANTS	107
Finding Your WOW and the Meaning of Life	109
White Blood Cells vs. Viruses	111
Forgiveness	113
Couple Therapy: Marital and Partner Relationships	117
Skills-based Model of Couple Therapy	119
Additional Issues in Couple Therapy	124
Anxiety and Depression	126
Panic Attacks	127
Obsessive-compulsive Disorder (OCD)	130
Hoarding	132
Social Anxiety	134
PTSD: Post-traumatic Stress Disorder	137
Adult ADHD and Uncluttering Your Home and Workplace	140

Summary	**143**

Appendix

Family as a Country — Case Study: Chris	145
Street Games	148
Figure 8: Make the Best of It	156
Figure 9: It's not HAT, it's FAD	157
Figure 10: Do You Suffer from HAT?	158
Figure 11: Stay Calm and Think on Your Feet	159
Figure 12: Three Steps for Confronting Anxiety, Frustration, Anger, and Stressful Situations	160
Skill Drill 1: Handling Teasing	160
Skill Drill 2: Being Positive	162
Figure 13: Positive Self-Thoughts	164
Figure 14: Be a Positive Person	165
Figure 15: Look for the Good	166
Figure 16: If You Had Fun, You Won	167
Figure 17: There are No Failures	168
Skill Drill 3: Why Did You Do That?	169
Figure 18: Don't Worry	171
Figure 19: Worrying Does Not Take Away Tomorrow's Troubles	172
Figure 20: To Overcome Your Fears	173
Social Skills Groups	174
Figure 21: Planning a Social Event	175
Figure 22: Socialized Child	176
Managing Children with ADHD	178
The Management of Adult Attention-deficit/Hyperactivity Disorder: Uncluttering Your Home and Workplace	186
Figure 23: Uncluttering Room	190
Figure 24: How is Your Business?	194

References   195

About the Author   196

Volume One
Childhood Issues and Interventions

The Family as a Country Model

Upon meeting a family in crisis, with children out of control and the relationship between parents strained to the limit, it was so important to respect their pain and struggle. They came to me, arms open and desperate for help. They needed to feel hopeful from the first contact. This began with the first phone call and certainly after the first session. I attempted to keep this in mind always and develop methods to ease the family into feeling confident in their ability to face issues and bring about changes. Knowledge and sincerity must be conveyed. As a therapist, a bond is created where, in a sense, you are joining their family. This is an extremely heavy emotional burden to bear. I, however, found this experience both rewarding and motivating for my work.

The **Family as a Country** model was a way to collect and organize the vast amount of information and variables available when beginning to assess what was going on with respect to the children when a new family came to see me. It was a way to be thorough. It helped to avoid missing essential details and becoming overly focused on minimal perspectives. When a child was brought to my attention, they brought their family, school, social, and biological worlds with them. Issues in all these areas interacted and combined, resulting in the child's behavior. Treatment was needed across many dimensions. In my view, I just couldn't fix a child and return them to an environment that had not also adjusted.

A demonstration of this concept is available in the Appendix "Case Study: Chris." Page 145

I began my assessment in **three stages**.

In the first session, I saw the child with the parent(s) together. The goal of this session was to interview the child. Having the parent present helped the child relax. I asked the child directly about their interests: school, friends, family, and health. To encourage the child's participation and develop rapport, I tried to limit talking to a parent about their child in front of the child. During the initial intake phone call, I would take at least fifteen minutes asking questions to give me some background regarding the reasons for referral.

With respect to teenagers, I often saw them first without the parent for most of the first session. This was done to facilitate rapport. Teens tend to be emotionally reactive. They needed to feel that I wanted to hear their side of the story. Indeed, if the teen and I could not bond, they would often refuse to attend further sessions. The goal was to begin my work without an intense teen-parent emotional disruption. I was careful to avoid seeming to be an agent solely of the parent. I was also very aware of the teens' attempts to bias me against their parents.

In the second session, I saw the child alone and conducted some mild psychological testing, such as figure drawings and a sentence completion test. Tests can at times reveal levels of disorder, such as psychosis and organicity. They may also reveal important emotional needs for that child. I found that this brief, non-invasive testing helped ease the child into a talking relationship and facilitated trust and rapport.

In the third session, I conducted a lengthy parent conference without the child or children present. Many times, parents would want to see me first and explain the child's problems before asking me for advice. I would explain that I could give general advice, but I still needed to see the child to offer more specific advice. I collected any medical and psycho-educational reports they had but often only reviewed them after I made my first two sessions of observation. At the parent conference, I began by showing them the **Family as a Country** diagram. See Fig. 1 (Page 21).

I explained that there were four sections of the country for intervention I wanted to address.

1. The Government: Needs of the Parents.
2. The Citizens: Needs of the Children
3. The System of Law and Order (that supports the country)
4. The System of Love and Attention (in the country)

When life in the country does not feel right, cooperation is down, and arguing is increasing at all levels, then it is time for someone in the country to call a time out. Just like a coach or player on a team, a time out is called to stop, assess, and correct the situation. Disorder is taught to be a signal that the country is in trouble. The process of correcting begins by working through the four sections of the country. Often, each section needs some adjusting. The focus is on problem solving and not blame.

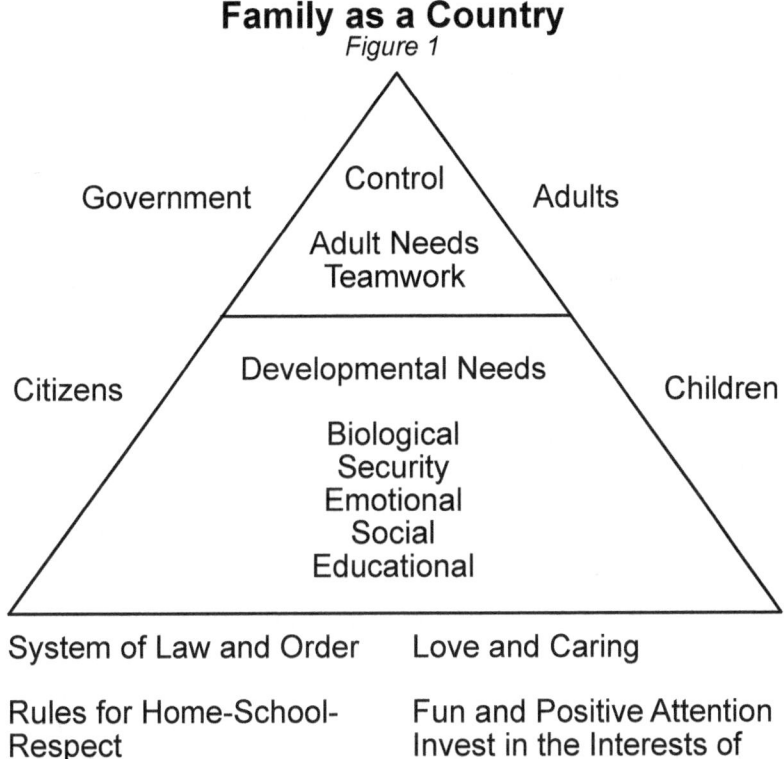

Family as a Country
Figure 1

The Government: Needs of the Parents

The first level of intervention places the needs of the parents at the top of the country as they are the government. They need to be in charge. They would become my co-therapists. It begins by asking the adults how they are doing as a couple and as individuals. Are they working as a team — one voice, one plan, "we" the parents? Is the couple still friends? Lovers? Is there a hot or cold war? It is particularly important to examine marital issues, but each adult or member of the government also has their own set of emotional needs, interests, and desires. Is a member of the government burned out, in crisis, or have they lost their own sense of identity? Many times, parents wear so many hats that, over time, they forget their own names. Burnout yields anger and depression. Often, adults who are in conflict emotionally take their feelings out on the family. It is easy to get angry at demanding and needy children or a spouse. Overreactions with discipline, or withdrawing from love and positive attention, are danger signals.

Raising children always tests our own struggles to grow up. Accepting less attention while sharing stress is a challenge of maturity. It is impossible to address our own needs all of the time. Teamwork and adjusting from a "me first" perspective to one based on "our" needs is necessary. It is especially important to view life as **our** cooking, cleaning, laundry, finances, jobs, health, extended families, and children, as well as **our** time together and apart. It is a time for planning and accepting that often, during the child-rearing years, the individual gets fewer of their needs, interests, and desires fulfilled than when they were single and less burdened by responsibilities. I liked to use the "pizza theory" to highlight this point. When you are single, you can enjoy the whole pie. Later, when you marry, you share half the pie with your spouse. As children come along, maybe you get to enjoy a slice!

More open planning or problem solving needs to be emphasized rather than fault-finding and blame. Helping each other to destress both together and individually is important. Exploring each other's parenting strengths and skills is more effective, such as who is more sensitive to love issues and who is stronger at discipline.

It is extremely important to look at pre-family expectations. A major problem I often found related to the parents' own childhood experiences going unresolved. Parents can repeat what they experienced with their own parents — even if there were conflicts and issues. For example, a person growing up in a home that was lacking in love may, as an adult, have problems knowing how to feel and give love to their spouse and children.

A country with parents who are not a solid government places too much control in the hands of the citizens/children who are not ready for self-rule. When the government is functioning well, calmness settles throughout the country and the citizens are far less anxious.

Many times when I began the adult assessment, parents avoided talking about their adult needs and jumped straight into telling me about their child's behavior. This was a defense that needed to be addressed. If the government is in danger of falling, then the country is going to fall as well. I would point out that my treatment approach was not to fix children but rather to treat systems. I always stressed that changes are often needed at many levels.

I helped the parents accept that children do not come equipped with a parenting instruction manual. Most parents base their approaches to parenting on what was modeled from their parents. Accepting parenting education is not an admission of failure but rather a constructive approach to growth and maturity.

The government/parents are expected to set up and enforce rules, set standards and values, and minister to the needs of the children/country. This is remarkably like how our own USA government works. A well-functioning government allows citizens to focus more time and energy on their personal needs. A government in disarray overloads the citizens emotionally, therefore increasing anxiety levels and feelings of insecurity. In my Family as a Country model I explained that, unlike the USA, a family/country is not a democracy. The government is not elected. Parents have been appointed by nature and will be held accountable by law for the actions of their children. Parents need to stay in control while the children grow up.

During this governing process, children need to feel loved and protected. Removing love for punishment should never happen. It is also important that children have some sense of non-abusive fear and apprehension of their parents. Children are extremely curious and will always test limits. They are especially curious about what is on the proverbial "other side of the fence." Without any fear of consequences, they will go too far and find themselves in situations beyond their abilities to handle. They need to have a concern and understanding that bad behavior will not be tolerated, and there will be consequences when rules are broken. Then, with a reasonable sense of apprehension, they may be more mindful when they test limits not to stray too far from safety.

As citizens of the United States of America, most people have a respect for following the rules and obeying the law. What stops someone from rushing past the window of a jewelry store, smashing it, and grabbing a handful of diamonds? It is a fear of the consequences. The law, for the most part, is fair and predictable in its application. We, as citizens, are fearful of being arrested and placed in jail. Without this concern, we would be living in a lawless, out-of-control society.

Parents I counseled were instructed how to enforce rules without being mean. I want very much to empower parents to be confident and fair but not abusive to their country/family. It is always important to stress that this is a teaching model rather than a blame/fault-finding model. If rules are not enforced at least 80-90% of the time, then the citizens take advantage and get into trouble by going way beyond reasonable boundaries. The citizens also need to trust that the government/parents will acknowledge and reward good, appropriate behavior. Even if the government is split, as with divorce or if only one parent is available due to issues like the death of a spouse, it is still important that the adult(s) remain in control.

As I assessed the government, I found out about the strength of the parents' relationship, parenting points of view, and special needs of parents regarding health, employment, family history, and current distractions. I looked for strengths, such as peer support, stress reduction, and openness to learning, and searched for weaknesses, such as infidelity, substance abuse, and financial stress.

Take care of your adult needs together. Be loving, fair, and consistent. The "government" stays in control.

It was especially important that the parents understood they were to be my co-therapists. Only together did we have any hope of helping the children. This meeting typically took a few hours as it was necessary to forge this bond. Allowing for ample time is necessary in that it can be highly emotional for the parents to face this challenge. Parents in distress will misunderstand their child's needs, and over- or underreact within the System of Law and Order, as well as within the System of Love and Attention.

As a session reached conclusion, I always gave my clients specific instructions, offering structure and skills which they could apply. The first set of skills they received were parenting tools. Understanding the application of these tools is essential at this stage of intervention. Parents require a sense of empowerment, knowing there are tools that can help them feel confident in taking control of the issues. Parents were given a handout to review at home.

See Fig. 2 below.

Parenting Tools
Figure 2

1. BIOLOGY
2. MODELING
3. CONSISTENCY OF RULES
4. LOVE
5. REFLECTIVE LISTENING
6. PROBLEM SOLVING

REASONING IS THE LEAST EFFECTIVE APPROACH

Parenting Tools

Parents have **six tools** to work with to help them be focused and more effective:

    1. Biology: Always be aware of the biological issues and needs of both the children and the parents.
    2. Modeling: Children learn by copying what they see.

3. Consistency of the Rules: Consistency helps the child know what they need to accomplish to get what they want. Inconsistency yields inconsistent compliance and increased frustration.

4. Love and Attention: Children gain security and positive self-esteem from the attention they receive. Poor attention or harsh comments can cause considerable negative, long-term consequences. Children more easily accept fair discipline when it is balanced with love and positive attention. Consistency of the rules and love and attention are the foundations that support the Family as a Country model. See Fig. 1 (Page 21)

5. Reflexive Listening. Parents need to learn to understand the real messages being expressed by a child's comments and behaviors. Overreacting to initial actions and words can often lead to missing the more important issues.

6 Problem Solving. Parents should seek solution-focused actions rather than obsessing on blame and negativity. The emphasis should be on teaching new ways of thinking and behavioral skills.

Throughout this book, I will be addressing various aspects of these four parenting tools.

As parental issues are revealed, parents need to engage in their own individual or couple therapies. Where possible, I worked with parents as well as the children. This was a modified family therapy approach: child, adult, couple, and family. Rather than splinter the family among many other clinicians, I found it more effective to work all aspects of the country. This allowed me to have one set of directions and focus. It also helped by not bringing in conflicting approaches that could confuse the members of the country. At times I brought the family together for sessions. It was also essential to have individual and/or couple sessions to work on issues.

At the start of parent therapies, I continued collecting background histories. I looked for parenting skills, biological markers, parenting generational patterns, educational levels, past therapies, cultural and religious viewpoints, and current stressors such as health, money, and employment. Once my assessment was complete, I proceeded to teach the government/parents how to understand and address the needs of their citizens/children.

Work on your parenting tools!

The Citizens: Needs of the Children

It is particularly important for parents to have a clear understanding of where their kids are developmentally, and to understand what to expect from them at different stages of development/aging. Children have needs, interests, and desires. Their needs change at different stages of development.

Parenting is work. It is a job that can become overwhelming. I find it strange that parents seem to forget what it feels like to grow up. They lose sight or awareness of how hard it is to go through growing up. This makes it difficult for them to have empathy for the struggles their own children are going through. It appears that, once they become parents, they often fall into following the parental script they had learned from their own parents. If your parents modeled a good script, then you are in luck. But parents I worked with often had poor role models, and as much as they said, "I would never raise my kids like the way my parents raised me," they usually followed the same old script.

I looked at kids from three stages: **the Age of Discovery, the Age of Opinion, and Teenage Thinking**.

These stages are the terms I put together to help simplify for parents the demands and expectations that are typically found at different times in a child's life. I tried hard to keep it simple and direct. Trying to explain complex personality and developmental stages is often way over the pay grade of the government.

Stage One: The Age of Discovery Child

The Age of Discovery years are ages zero-to-seven. These children are most concerned with exploring their worlds through the various senses. They are busy collecting information and learning to navigate life as they know it. Life during these years is usually focused on two interactive, major need issues: **biology and security**.

What do I mean by the **biological nature** of children? Children are not born blank. They come equipped with many biologically-based traits such as how bright they are, how well their sensory nervous systems function, what will naturally interest them, and personality traits and dispositions. Often these personality traits are inherited. When I would explain heredity, I often heard parents say, "See? He is just like you (or your brother, grandfather, etc.)." Knowing that the family trait is inborn can help a parent understand what their child may be going through. How the parent has been affected by these traits is especially important to reveal. Perhaps one can ask a parent how they coped with these same issues. I tried to evoke empathy and insight rather than place blame, which is more often the tendency with many governments in disarray.

Some children are born to be very bright and have the potential for higher education, while others may have limitations. There are children whose talents lie in their mechanical abilities and hands-on technical skills. Some children have issues with learning disabilities, or attention and focusing with or without hyperactivity or impulsivity. Some children will be born with easygoing natures while others may have the tendency to become oppositional. Kids are often born as mirror images of the family tree. The tendencies for anxiety, depression, OCD, ADHD, and addiction run in families. Two or more children in a family may inherit different dispositions. One child may be calm and easygoing while the other is demanding and easily frustrated. Too often I have heard parents say, "Why can't you be like your sibling?" to the acting-out child.

There are also children who have biologically-based issues that stem from prenatal problems or birth trauma. Biological issues may dominate a child's life at all stages and must be taken into consideration when planning treatment in each stage. The more severe the biological issue, the greater the need to make significant adjustments.

The Age of Discovery child's attention span is noticeably short. They are focused on what is happening right now and cannot bridge time. Time frames are extremely limited. It is what is happening immediately that counts most. They are not looking beyond the moment to what will happen later in the day or week. Discovery kids want immediate responses for their needs.

It is important to note that temper tantrums are a normal expression of frustration by a young child. When they occur, it is a time to remove them from the situation, remove the object from them, or distract them. Temper tantrums are common and should be tolerated. Permit them to run their course, provided the tantrums do not allow the child to gain the object of desire, or cause injury to others or themselves. Dangerous actions should result in restraint. I will address proper restraint techniques later.

It is also important to note that, at this early stage, the typical brain of a young child lacks the ability for reasoning and logic to understand family rules, make complex decisions, understand what you are saying, or see consequences beyond the immediate time period. It takes many years to accumulate experiences to understand the world. We cannot just upload all we have learned over our lifetimes into the child at birth and expect them to start from where we left off. It usually takes at least twenty years for children to grow up. Every generation must, as it is said, "reinvent the wheel."

The slow process of developmental maturity can account for why it is so difficult for people to learn from history. A child focuses mostly on the present, while history fades into the background. The lessons that can be learned could be missed. The same can be said about a society. While we focus on current events, lessons from our history are ignored. As a result, we keep repeating the same mistakes, as in the case of wars.

At this stage, parents often begin making a critical mistake of trying to reason with their child as their primary form of discipline, wasting a lot of time and energy. Children love to debate. If you keep talking, they will continue trying to find a way around the rules. Reasoning with kids should be reserved for much later years, often when they are paying for their own wants and desires. Parents can briefly express their reasons for their own actions, yet it is not what they say but what they do that counts. Actions always speak louder than words! Yelling and screaming will result in resentment and will come back at the parent in later years when the child models the behavior. A screaming parent is most likely not dealing with their own issues such as fatigue, hunger, illness, or unresolved conflicts. They are not asking the first question: "Is the government having a problem?"

When life with children, be it at home or in the community, is getting off track, stop! Check yourself, and then think biology. Observe what is happening with the child and the adults that is related to biology: fatigue, hunger, illness, discomfort, or inborn biological issues.

Keep in mind that, due to the course of busy daily life, I consider a 20% "out-of-control" rate as a baseline in most families. These types of events may reflect issues with time management, misplaced objects like keys and shoes, missing biological cues linked to illness, fatigue, or hunger, a breakdown in teamwork, or not taking time for stress reduction. Anything higher means we are missing a critical issue or need.

Although Age of Discovery kids will develop words to express their needs, they lack a more mature awareness of the context of the situation. They cannot easily express verbally what is troubling them. They can tell you they want a toy but cannot interpret whether it is the right time or place, or be aware of the needs of those around them. When confronted, they become frustrated and often cry. It is their normal, primitive way of saying, "I don't like what you decided for me." When they get upset, they get a surge of adrenaline that energizes their frustration. I will say more on this when discussing anger management.

At this point, I want to emphasize that attempting to reason with a child, especially one in the throes of an adrenaline rush, will only extend the tantrum and often results in a parental tantrum. It is "no means no" or "yes" when it is appropriate, and then moving on from the tantrum. By attempting to reason with the child, a parent is showing their vulnerability to them; this becomes a button the child pushes in the next stages: the Age of Opinion and Teenage Thinkers.

Reasoning with children at all stages tends to be ineffective.

What does **Security** mean? Is a child's world safe, trusting, and comforting? Is the world around them consistent with respect to routines? Are basic biological needs, such as hunger or thirst, treatment of illness, or calming sensory distress, being addressed? Does the government help in calming a child who is distressed, such as picking up a baby or toddler and hugging them to help them feel safe? Children instinctively sense fear and danger as well as safety. In this early stage, they cannot identify the source of a loud noise or parents fighting. The child cries out to signal danger. "Help me somebody! Pay attention!" It is an inborn trait found throughout the animal kingdom.

Parents who are in distress often pass on their own anxiety and tension through the manner of their touch or lack of touch, through sensory overload, and by ignoring a child's biological needs. Trying to force a child into adjusting to their busy schedule will often result in stressed out kids. I have seen situations where a child is rushed to an early drop off for day care, then transferred to school, then taken to an afternoon daycare program before finally arriving home in the early evening, only to be met by an exhausted parent trying to rush dinner and bedtime.

Another example of stress transfer I have seen involves taking young children shopping or to the grocery store. Most younger children cannot tolerate the sensory overload and have limits to their patience. The parents complain that the acting-out child does not understand. They blame the child rather than the child's natural inability to be flexible. Planning must consider a child's inborn nature and biological issues. It may be necessary to do a quick grocery shopping for essentials and save the larger, staple shopping for when your partner can watch the kids.

It is particularly important to adjust life schedules to the child's inborn, biological nature.

The Age of Discovery child's sense of security is highly tied to parental emotional states. Problems occurring at the government level will pervade the entire country, affecting all citizens.

A child will often perceive one of the parents to be the **security parent** — the parent who will take care of their biological and security needs. In our culture, we have often placed Mom at the center of the child's security needs. They attach very closely and seek her out in times of need.

I used to believe that this role was instinctive to the mother-child relationship, that a biological attachment began nine months prior to birth and was the mother's singular role. I have since seen many stay-at-home fathers who took on the nurturing role and became the recognized security parent. The security parent often sets the tone, pace, and routines that the young child comes to expect and rely upon. Consistency is helpful for security. It is the security parent who often needs to take the lead when handling the Age of Discovery child. I have also seen nannies and grandparents become security-parent figures, especially when both parents are working and out of the home frequently.

When the **non-security parent** or working parent comes home, it is particularly important to follow the direction of the security parent. Rushing in and disrupting routines confuses the young child and increases stress reactions. There is an especially important role for the working parent as support and relief for the stressed-out security parent. If partners disagree with respect to roles and direction, then it is best to have discussions away from the purview of the child, while taking into consideration time to defuse their own emotional overreaction. Accepting professional intervention to mediate these differences would be an excellent bonding experience for parents.

I like to use the following example to highlight this issue: Consider that a hospital often has three nursing care shifts. Doctors often see most patients during the remarkably busy day shift and leave instructions for patient care with the head nurse. The head nurse then needs to pass on instructions for care to the next shift's head nurse to have continuity of care. This will repeat upon the third shift's arrival. The day shift head nurse is like the security parent. Each succeeding shift takes its cues from that head nurse and passes information along.

Biology and security are basic primary needs.

Social Behavior of the Age of Discovery Child

Regarding **social needs,** the Age of Discovery child often plays in parallel to other children. They are not so in need of play dates or having best friends. Parents should not become obsessed with the number of friends one child has compared to another child. In the early years, what leads to friendships are the relationships of the children's parents. They often bring their young children together to play.

Discovery kids are very into their parents. They lack the ability to understand complex play. If you watch a bunch of five-year-old children on a soccer field and the ball goes in one direction, you'll most likely see twenty kids chasing after it, followed by twenty screaming parents trying to keep their child in their positions. At the same time, another group of kids may be picking grass and flowers, totally unaware of their circumstances while parents are shouting out instructions to engage in the play.

Playing with other children is important for learning about others. A play date should be small — two to three kids per session — and in short duration. Parents should model by playing along. Children left on their own to play will usually split off to isolated activities or get into conflicts.

Social activity will also greatly depend upon the child's inborn biological issues and personality traits. Some children are calm and confident, some shy and overwhelmed, and others breech boundaries and are overbearing. Plan play events around what your unique child can tolerate.

Children in the same family, as mentioned previously, can be quite different depending on their inherited qualities. Some will like sports, others will prefer music and art, while some will be interested in science and nature. Plan play activities around their innate interests. If the parent's natural interests differ from the child's, it is still especially important for the parent to learn how to play with the child. Play is a major bonding activity and can be very emotionally supportive. When a parent avoids the child because they don't play what the parent likes, it sends out a clear message of rejection. I have conducted many play sessions with parents and children. I would join the play and model how to stay emotionally involved. Over time, I would disengage and just observe and give feedback and positive reinforcement.

Interests and social preference will vary from child to child, even in the same family.

Discipline with the Age of Discovery Child

I again want to point out that reasoning with this young child is a waste of time! I suggest focusing more on **what** behavior is going on, **when** it is happening, **where** it occurs, **who** is around as well as the **consequences** that follow the behavior.

Parents can do much to help with discipline by managing **biology and the environment**. Many times, I have seen children acting out whose home environments were out of control. Scheduling was haphazard, biological needs were unmet, and there were "too many cooks" but no "executive chef" in charge.

I have worked with children who cannot eat on the parent's schedule. Their blood sugar levels drop and they become moody and anxious. Ask someone with diabetes; they know the feeling well. Some of these kids are better off eating more frequent, smaller meals. I have seen smiling parents pick up wild, angry children from school. The child had behaved well in school, but as soon as they got in the car "Dr. Hyde" emerged. Discipline, threats, or punishment made it worse. It turned out they were simply hungry! Often children do not eat enough at lunch due to distractions and mood. I instructed the parents to have a snack in the car, ready to pop in the child's mouth upon first sight. Five minutes later it was, "Hi Mom, glad to see you."

The same can be said when it comes to restaurants. Many children are very hungry upon arriving at the restaurant and cannot wait thirty minutes or more for food. When they are hungry, their sensory systems overload quickly. It may be helpful to either bring food along for the child to eat while you are waiting or, if you have a favorite neighborhood restaurant, to call ahead and place the order so it is ready when you arrive. In some cases, it is simply better not to go out if the child is not ready biologically.

Hunger may not be the only biological issue at play. Irritable children may also be ill or tired. Their attention spans are much shorter when they are tired. Young children cannot easily verbalize that they are not feeling well. They are not like adults who know when they are coming down with something. Their behavior sends a strong message that something biological may be in play.

Some children can also act out because of food sensitivities that make them hyper and oppositional. Some kids are born with sensitivities to food colorings and food additives. In addition, it could be milk, fruits, wheat, processed foods, sugars, or some other food that is particular to that child. An early work of Dr. Benjamin Feingold (1975), *Why Your Child is Hyperactive,* clearly highlights this issue. Another good resource is a book called *The Impossible Child* by Drs. Doris J. Rapp and Dorothy Bamberg (1986). What children eat could be why they are out of control.

Traditional allergy testing may not show all food sensitivities. When trying to determine if a child is having a food reaction, parents are asked to keep a detailed food log of what the child eats and their behavioral reactions thirty to sixty minutes later. Once a pattern emerges, the child is placed on a bland diet for two weeks and then certain foods are gradually reintroduced to narrow down the culprit.

In addition, what children eat in school needs to be recorded. I worked with children who had severe hyperactive and oppositional behavior in school. These kids were very sensitive to food colorings. In some cases, it turned out that some teachers were giving out snacks and treats high in food coloring as rewards. Children often like to share treats with each other at lunch, which could also present a problem.

Another group of children act up due to sensory overload. They may have auditory discrimination/processing problems. Some children cannot process sound very well. What may seem like normal sound could be too loud for them. Others cannot discern background sounds from foreground sounds. This could explain why they do not hear when a parent calls for them. Consider a typical house with all kinds of sounds in the background, such as TV, washing machines, someone talking on the phone, or even outside noises like cars and trucks, lawn mowers, etc. Trying to get a child's attention against all that sound could present quite a challenge. The parent might need to get closer and be within arm's length to have a chance to be heard. Auditory discrimination training for young children has been shown to have some beneficial effects to help with this problem.

Having played the drums in rock bands for fifty years, my ears are shot. My hearing is like what a child or person with ADHD experiences. Put me in a noisy room and all sounds blend. I struggle to pick out and follow conversations due to background noise. I also am unable to discern where sounds are coming from.

Another sensory issue that can contribute to disruptive behavior is tactile or touch sensitivity. For these children, their worlds become uncomfortable when they experience certain sensations on the skin. This can also result from temperature variations. I have seen children who love cold weather and comfortably wear shorts all winter long. This often drives parents crazy. Labels or tight-fitting clothing can also be annoying. Some children prefer long sleeves, even in summer heat. Some of the children I saw benefitted from sensory stimulation occupational therapy.

Another major source of distress is too much exposure to screens; TV, computers, and video games can overload the nervous systems of many children. Their brains get too much stimulation, and when it is time to stop the electronic activity, they go through a withdrawal stage of thirty or more minutes during which time they can become very agitated. I have often seen this problem when parents allow children to stay on the screens until the moment they must change to a new activity. There is no calming transition period, so they carry the overload into the next activity. This is a common experience with children acting out in the car when parents are rushing to the next event. Try to turn off screens twenty to thirty minutes before changing activities to allow for transition.

Young children have extremely limited memories to go along with their innate, short attention spans. When instructing a young child to do a task, keep it simple: "Go and get your blue sneakers." Too many instructions will be easily forgotten. With young children I sometimes used Post-it notes with drawings to give the child a concrete object to focus on to minimize distractions. They could easily carry the note along to remind themselves of the task. Discovery kids cannot follow a list or chart of responsibilities like the Age of Opinion child can.

When dealing with disciple issues, again, first think biology.

Managing the home **environment** is particularly important with young children. Age of Discovery kids cannot easily organize and sort toys. They may start to clean up but are often distracted by their short attention spans. They do not value the cost of a toy and may step on an expensive toy as easily as an inexpensive toy.

Don't let your home become TOYS-R-US 2! The last few generations of parents and grandparents (myself included) have had the means to indulge the toy cravings of our children and grandchildren. Marketing has manipulated both parents and kids into believing that the child must have this or that toy. I hate to say it (I sound so old), but when I was a child our imaginations were our best toys and means to occupy our leisure time. Making up games was the play excitement among the neighborhood kids. I have included a list of common street games we played in the appendix on Page 148.

Toys need to be kept at a controllable level. Packing up and rotating toys from season to season brings a rediscovery that will seem like getting new toys all over again. If too many toys are left around, they are not valued no matter what the cost was. Remember, Discovery kids do not understand value. To them, a toy is a toy regardless of the cost.

Toys, as well as electronic devices, need to be placed under parental control. This is important for two reasons: overstimulation and rule enforcement.

First, controlling access to toys helps avoid overstimulation. If a play area is overrun with toys, it will soon resemble a dump. Young children cannot easily put their toys away. They get distracted and their senses get overwhelmed. Then the child gets frustrated as well as the parent, who will eventually have to clean up the dump. Control over access to toys is a way of making life easier for everyone.

In addition to rotating toys, I recommend they be kept in a toy closet. The closet should include a lock to restrict access. When a child wishes to take out a toy, it should be required that some toys go back into the closet before new ones are removed. Keep bins in the closet in which to organize toys, e.g. blocks, cars, action figures. Place expensive toys on the highest shelves to be taken down and used under close parental/adult supervision.

It's a good idea to structure clean-up periods. At key times of the day, initiate clean-up time. Try to attach activities like watching TV or using other electronic devices to occur after cleaning up. Waiting for bedtime to do a major clean-up usually does not work well due to fatigue, and there are fewer motivational activities to hold over them.

Designate play-only areas. A child has a playroom but not the whole house. Do not let the toys spread out like weeds in a garden. Select adult/family areas that are off limits to play and toys.

Second, having an area or toy closet that can be locked will help to enforce rules when applying discipline. It is especially important that a parent be able to follow through at least 80-90% of the time when they have set a limit. Access to toys should be linked to rule following. A child with hidden caches of toys around the house does not feel the impact of a rule being enforced. Being sent to his or her room for misbehavior is meaningless if the room is full of toys. A child can be rewarded with access to the toy closet for good, appropriate behavior. A child with unlimited access to toys will learn to disregard the parents and the rules.

An inconsistent parent is only teaching the child to ignore what the parent says. **Children feel more secure when they know the government is in charge.** Consistency helps children learn what they need to do to be allowed access to toys without an emotional breakdown or tantrum.

Oppositional children will test every rule. It is particularly important to be at least 90% consistent in follow-through with them. These are the kids for whom the saying "give them an inch, they will take a mile" was made. They will try to find any way to bypass consequences. I have found that electronic devices need to have lock-out passwords, be locked in a closet, or for a lockout box to be installed over the outlet plug, such as with TV plugs. You must win these battles.

At times, allowing a child to experience natural consequences can be a better teacher than a meaningless lecture/argument. For example, rather than have a fight with the child to put their coat on because it is cold outside, allow the child to go out and feel the cold. Bring the coat along. Without a lecture or "I told you so," the cold child will most likely ask for the coat. If a parent argues over the coat, most oppositional kids would rather freeze than give in to their demand. How did we learn about cold? We got cold!

Avoid reasoning. Biology, a structured environment, and natural consequences matter more than words!

The Power of Positive Reinforcement with the Age of Discovery Child

These young children are not equipped for a rule-based system based on awareness of time, duration, and consequence. They focus on the more immediate or what is right in front of them. A rule-based system will be explained when I discuss the Age of Opinion child.

The principle of positive reinforcement notes that what is rewarding for one child is not the same for all children. It will take some effort to find what works for your child. A reward is used to encourage positive behavior. There are two types of positive reinforcers: primary and secondary.

Primary reinforcers are those that relate to biological states, particularly taste and touch, such as treats and hugs. Kids find these types of rewards very pleasing right from the get-go. Effective use of treats can shape up complex behaviors. Shaping is a process of starting to reward and prompting small approximation steps gradually towards more complex behavior. I have told parents many times that puppy training manuals are a good model for raising young children. Give a command or request, prompt the behavior both verbally and physically, followed by giving a small treat/reward. As time progresses, gradually expect more effort with less prompting to gain the treat. Combine the treat with hugs and praise.

Secondary reinforcers are activities that acquire a rewarding quality over time. Being able to watch TV or play with certain toys often are good rewards for the older Discovery child. Once a child acquires the desire for this type of activity, it can be used to shape behavior by requiring steps to be completed before gaining access. Try to use watching screens, TV or computer, as the last activity in a chain of behavioral requirements, such as dressing themselves, toileting, and eating their meal. "When you finish eating, then you can use the screen." "When you have gotten dressed, then you can have the toy." Too often I find parents awarding the screen privilege before the child has completed the necessary tasks. The parents then try to take the screen back, which results in a major tantrum.

The difference between rewards and bribery is important to understand. Rewards are earned for making effort. Access to toys and screens is the reward. Dangling bribes with promises of buying expensive toys for small amounts of behavior only teaches children to hold up their parents. They easily learn to demand a bigger and bigger bribe for continuing behavior. Presents like new toys should come for special holidays and birthdays, representing a message of love. Sometimes, when a special effort is made, the child can get an unexpected reward. They will appreciate the reward and feel good for being acknowledged for their extra effort.

Parents are always working for five years ahead. What they allow early on will become the norm at later stages and will be difficult to undo without severe emotional reactions.

> *Positive reinforcements teach new behaviors. Do not reason; stay calm and follow through. Shape up new skills in small steps.*

Restraint Techniques for Aggressive Behavior with the Age of Discovery Child

At times, young children will have aggressive and/or self-injurious temper tantrums. It will become necessary to gain control over them for the protection of themselves and others.

Biology is the primary issue to be addressed first. When anyone, no matter what age, becomes upset, a primitive defense mechanism is set off. It is the **fight-or-flight** response. The brain thinks something dangerous has occurred and prepares us to be able to meet the challenge. Chemical reactions occur almost instantly. Even babies cry out when startled. Oppositional kids, whom I refer to as "light switch kids," get energized quickly, as when one flips on a light switch — zero to 100 in the blink of an eye!

The primary chemical involved is adrenaline, a chemical that rushes into our bloodstream, giving us instant energy and strength. In times of danger, this can save our lives. When it surges in an inappropriate reaction, such as with angry tantrums, it can be extremely dangerous.

When the danger/frustration alarm goes off, our brain drops whatever we have been thinking about. Cognitive reasoning ceases while we focus on the danger. Muscles get tighter and breathing becomes faster. We take in less oxygen, which results in an inability for the brain to think about anything not relevant to the danger. Oxygen levels are especially important when dealing with imminent threats. As the body takes in less oxygen, the brain receives less oxygen. Our brains are oxygen sensitive, so much so that even a short period — four to six minutes — of no oxygen will result in death. We can restart a heart but not a brain. With less oxygen available to the brain due to muscle contraction and rapid breathing, the brain compensates by focusing only on what may be necessary to control the danger.

To further understand, this example may be helpful: Imagine yourself crossing a street. Suddenly, you see a bus coming at you. You jump back quickly, your heart is racing, and your leg and arm muscles are tight. Your only thought is on staying alive. How quickly did this occur? Are you still thinking of all the things that had been on your mind previously? If you are reading this, then your reaction time was excellent! Yet, if you didn't notice the bus, the emergency alarm would not go off and your reaction might be too late. In life, a mere second or two can make a big difference.

Our brains cannot easily determine if an alarm is a **real** emergency or a **false** alarm. Firemen at the firehouse, when the alarm goes off, rush forward into the danger zone preparing for the potential fire. They do not know if it is real or not. They respond to every alarm as if it is real, even if the last one was false. They cannot afford to ignore any alarm. As they rush about, they stop thinking of their families, vacation plans, etc. and focus only on saving lives. Our brains react to alarms in the same way.

The Safety Zone

Remember, the Age of Discovery child has limited reasoning ability to begin with. During times of distress, reasoning is further diminished. Trying to reason with an out-of-control child — or even with an out-of-control adult — is often only going to aggravate the situation. Older children, age seven and up, can learn to use the physical reaction of an adrenaline rush as a signal to start a coping response, such as stepping back to a **Safety Zone**. The Safety Zone is a place for the adrenaline/energy to be safely discharged. The first step in anger management is to step back to a Safety Zone rather than step forward into a danger zone. In the danger zone, adrenaline reactions can increase and a prolonged fight can occur.

With the young Age of Discovery child, we will need to create a Safety Zone. This will at times involve physical restraint. Holding an out-of-control child is not abuse or even a poor role-modeling of aggression. It is important to protect the child and the environment around them. If properly done, physical restraint can be a way of containing biology and bringing a child to security. The young child cannot restrain themselves. They cannot easily find their Safety Zone. Continuous, out-of-control behavior episodes will damage the child's self-image, family relationships, and social standing.

Back in 1980, I was working at a New York State Developmental Center. It was an inpatient hospital for people with severe mental limitations. These patients could be extremely aggressive. The staff was afraid to get too actively involved with treatment for fear of being hurt. I was given specialized training by New York State as an instructor in safe, non-abusive, physical restraint. I taught staff how to intervene physically to safeguard the patients and themselves. As staff began to apply these new skills, the patients became more manageable and the staff more willing to become involved with treatment.

At the same time, these procedures were being adopted for aggressive, out-of-control, oppositional children. For over forty years I taught parents how to safely restrain their children. When parents followed these guidelines, they were able to gain control over their child's behavior and help the child feel safe and protected.

When the aggressive response begins and the adrenaline switch is activated, parents need to respond quickly to physically intervene. The biggest problem occurs when parents start reasoning and go through many warnings. The longer the delay, the stronger the child becomes. Adrenaline is powerful. Our eventual goal is to get the child to a Safety Zone but, while the body is out of control, restraint will be the primary Safety Zone. **I must stress that restraint is to be used only for immediate danger.** If a child can lie on the floor and scream without presenting an immediate danger to itself or others, then let them.

Steps for Physical Restraint

Step 1: The alarm goes off. A child raises an arm at you or a sibling, an object has been thrown, or a table has been turned over. Do not rush forward into the front of the child's body. Staying in front will lead to you getting kicked, bitten, punched, or your hair pulled. Quickly grab one arm near the wrist and spin the child around while gaining control of the other arm. Cross the arms across the child's front while you stand behind. Use just enough force to keep your grip. Control your own impulse to vent your adrenaline into the child.

Step 2: Keep your head against the child's back to avoid being head butted. Keep moving the child in order to keep them from kicking you. Do not let them set their feet.

Step 3: Most young children will go down to the floor. Continue going down to the floor with the child face down under your body. Keep control of the arms. Lie across the child's back with your stomach over their back. Place your leg across their legs. Remember not to place your entire weight on the child but just enough to keep them confined.

Step 4: Prepare to ride out the storm. Adrenaline often requires five to ten minutes to be discharged. When you are holding the child, they will have an increased adrenaline rush which can take longer to abate. Be prepared to hear some of the worst screams, threats, and "I hate you" comments you have yet to hear. It is the adrenaline talking — they do not mean it.

They are venting the adrenaline and under your body is the safest place. You are taking control over an out-of-control, dangerous body. Some kids will scream that they cannot breathe, however, if they can speak then they can breathe. Someone truly choking cannot verbalize words.

Step 5: Do not reason or argue or bargain with your child. They will promise you anything to be let go. While you have them in control, you should continue to work on your own calming down. Notice your breathing. Breathe slowly and loudly so the child may eventually catch up to the pace of your breath. Hum a tune, and keep yourself composed.

Step 6: Keep holding the child until you feel the tension running out of them. Be careful not to let go until you are sure the child has released the adrenaline. Letting go too soon can lead to a false positive and the child may resume their tantrum. You want to exhaust the adrenaline rush. Take a few more minutes holding this position until no further energy is invested in fighting you.

Step 7: As the tension releases, slowly bring the child into a sitting position in your lap. Keep control of your grip and remain behind the child. Start quietly telling the child, "Everything is fine, I love you. I am not angry at you; I am just helping you calm down." Often the child is sorry and will respond well to a hug, seeking security.

Step 8: Try to take them to their bed and have them lie down while you slowly massage and hug them lovingly. Once everyone is calm, go back to the rest of your day. It is important to follow through with the rule. Do not let the child have what they wanted prior to the tantrum.

The first few times a parent goes through restraining their child will be very emotional. Often, a parent feels so badly that they give in to future threats out of guilt. This is only going to teach the child that they can bully the parent. I mentioned earlier that children need to have some sense of intimidation or fear of their parents to feel safe. They learn that control is security. A parent or teacher who is firm and not mean will be more respected than an easily manipulated or intimidated parent or teacher.

I have had oppositional children test me right away in my office. I had to restrain them. I did not allow them to continue hurting their parent or sibling, or destroying my office. Initially, they screamed "I hate you!" but, after they calmed down and we settled into positive play, they became my best friend. They then knew my tolerance and limits and had a clearer understanding of my rules. They trusted that, if they lost control, I would be able to help them regain it. Furthermore, I encouraged parents to take some time to practice the restraint techniques with a partner before engaging their child.

While it is especially important to be the initial Safety Zone for an out-of-control child, it is also important to continue developing an **alternative Safety Zone**. During quiet times, role-play with your child where they can go when they are upset. Take turns pretending you are angry. Practice screaming into a pillow, squeezing nerf balls, listening to music, or even using a drum pad to work out the energy. Get them to be aware of how their body feels when they are angry: arms and legs tight, chest tight, breathing fast. Reward them for this role-playing.

For some children, a Safety Zone is just a place where they can go and be quiet. The bedroom can be a primary place for a **Calm Out.** The goal is to learn that the first step in controlling anger is to step back to a Safety Zone. The child can go to this area to discharge anger. It may take minutes up to half an hour to get past the adrenaline reaction. Recall that the bedroom should not be a place overloaded with toys and expensive objects. It should be a quiet place to induce relaxation and sleep.

There is an important distinction between **Time Out** and a **Calm Out**. I do not call stepping away a Time Out — I call it a Calm Out. "Calm Out" focuses on the body message as a signal to begin self-control. Too often, "Time Out" means punishment, and the message of body-awareness for self-control is missed.

Parents should model going to a Safety Zone when they are upset. Prepare an area in the house where you can go to discharge your energy. It may be a place where you can hit your bed or a bean bag chair, or scream into your pillow. Children learn from modeling what we do. Do not be unnerved when you are out of control and the child reminds you to go to your Safety Zone. A clearer mind can administer the rules better than a mind on an adrenaline rush.

Once parents have used the restraint procedures about five or six times and have practiced the role-playing, they will have a tool to redirect the child more quickly to the bedroom Safety Zone. As the out-of-control child is met by taking control of their arms from behind them, you can ask, "Do you want to go to your Safety Zone?" If they say yes, then, without letting go, walk them to their bed and, while still holding them, place them face down onto the bed. Be sure they are not too overloaded with adrenaline before you release the arms. A false positive will escalate quickly. It still may be necessary to have a few more take-down-to-the-floor type of restraint episodes. The oppositional child will always test to see if you can still be trusted to stop them. Continually strive to remain calm, give positive praise, and reward the child for learning how to do a Calm Out.

Proper restraint and developing Safety Zones help the child feel safe and secure. Teach them how to appropriately express anger.

Stage Two: The Age of Opinion Child

Age of Discovery children have spent the last five to seven years observing the lay of the land. These kids primarily require immediate responses from their parents. They have constructed a map based on how consistent their parents have been. Now they are ready to take that map and run with it. **I like to refer to children between the ages of seven and twelve as Age of Opinion children.**

The brain of the Age of Opinion child has made a major leap in development. They can bridge time and stay focused on short- and long-term needs, interests, and desires. They are now able to delay reinforcement. They can be held accountable for behaviors that happened earlier in the day with consequences later in the day or week. It is time to move to a rule-based, privilege-earning model of discipline. They can now be expected to take on certain jobs and responsibilities.

These children are even more invested in arguing and controlling their parents. Do not argue or reason with them. They know all your vulnerable places and will try to exploit them. The longer they have you in an argument, the odds increase that they will eventually get their way. If you lose your composure, they will gladly blame you for why they did not get what they wanted. "It is your fault you yelled at me." Stay 80-90% consistent with the rules. You may be wrong with your judgments sometimes, but, if you are inconsistent, you will make many more mistakes with judgment.

Age of Opinion kids, aside from growing, will remain relatively stable with biology. They have less emotional variability due to biological factors, unlike the hormonally charged Teenage Thinkers. There are still in-born biological issues that will continue to need attention, such as ADHD. Two new needs, however, begin to dominate this child: **sense of self and social involvement**.

They now have opinions based on self-awareness **(sense of self)** or what they like. For example, they now have preferences such as "I like these shows," or toys, foods, places, etc. From now on, they will always have an opinion.

These children begin to strongly attach to adults to develop a role model of expected female and/or male images. Often, when Mom has been the primary security parent, Dad now has a big role as the self-esteem parent. They mostly spent time in the company of Mother while Father often worked outside the home and was therefore less visible. They have learned a great deal about women during the early years. Now they seek out Dad's attention. They start to pull away from Mom, feeling more confident and seeking independence. "I do not need a mommy as much to tell me what to do." They now seek Dad's approval. A father's attention can lift a child, but lack of attention or harsh reactions can crush the young, emerging self-image. Mom remains in the security role. They quickly seek her out when they become anxious. Boys look up to Dad to get an idea of how men behave, and girls seek him out to learn what to expect from men. Girls will look more closely to Mom again in the teen years as they undergo significant biological changes.

With families that have the father as the security parent, it will be Mom who is in the provider role. Either way, the children try to find a consistent image of how their role-model parents behave and think, and what they value and believe. Reflect for a moment on how or why you grew up having certain attitudes, religious beliefs, or political viewpoints. Even though you can choose what to believe, these values often are set by the parent role models.

Social needs begin to blossom. Children seek out friends based on similar interests, such as sports, music, arts, and science. Some children become leaders of others due to a charismatic personality trait, while others become followers. It is a time for parents to help their children develop confidence in their own innate interests. As mentioned previously, parents need to show support by playing and interacting with their children through their child's interests, even if it is not the parent's interest. Children in a family will often differ from each other based upon innate personality traits. In a family with many children, interaction can become quite a challenging task.

I came from a family whose parents were holocaust survivors. My parents rarely played with us. I had no role models of how a parent plays with children. This became an issue for me when raising my own children. My two sons were born fourteen months apart. They were raised in the same household but are quite different in interests and personality. One child enjoyed sports and music and could handle competition. I loved to relax with sports, so it was easier to play with him. The other son was a science and nature kid and less comfortable with competition. That was not my play/relaxing activity. I had to be willing to learn how to share in his science and nature interests and have more patience. As previously discussed, this issue is common with parents who had poor role models. They do not know how to play with their children. In treating this issue, I often conducted many family play-therapy sessions.

Interestingly, within my psychology practice, I did not initially work with children until I had learned how to play with my own children. Learning to play with them opened up a second chance at childhood for me. It was fun to read comics, share sci-fi books, take nature hikes, create indoor tennis games, make movies, and create silly bedtime stories. These activities have remained a cornerstone of my relationship with my now-adult children, and have created great memories that have been passed down.

Unlike Teenage Thinkers, the Age of Opinion child is still centered in family. They want friends, but are not obsessed with social relationships yet. It is a great time for families to bond through trips, hobbies, and interests. Parents who do a good job staying connected with children at this stage are setting up a closeness that will survive the more turbulent teen years. Children will stay closer to instilled values and rebel less. Distant or harsh parents are compelling their teens to seek values from their peers — more often from other angry and disconnected children.

> *Self and social needs begin to become important to the Age of Opinion child. Parents tuning into these needs build strong and positive bridges to the future.*

The System of Law and Order: The "Choose to Earn Privileges" Discipline Model

There are individual needs that the government and citizens must address. In addition, as with any country, there needs to be a structure that holds the country together. I call this the **Choose to Earn Privileges** model. **See Fig. 3 on next page.**

Discipline and responsibility development can be taught from a rule-based home model. Age of Opinion children need to learn to take on more responsibilities. Rewards, or privileges as I call them, are earned. Children gain privileges based on complying with three areas of responsibility: **Home, School, and Respect**. There are chores and requirements within each area. The child chooses to earn or not earn their privileges. As with adult jobs, it is a choice to work or not work. No one makes a person work. It is not a take-away model in that no one takes away salary or wages; they are earned through effort. Similarly, it is a positive approach to let children make choices and accept consequences.

As always, reasoning and arguing are not necessary. Consistency with the rules and consequences is the trick. Children are given an idea of reasonable behaviors they are required to perform at least 80% of the time to earn their privileges. They are given control to attain them. I point out again that it is like having a paid job. If you do not work, you do not get paid — you get fired. We cannot "fire" our kids until they're eighteen, the predominant age of consent, but we do not have to pay them if they don't work. This Choose to Earn approach makes attaining a privilege a reward for good effort. A punishment model of take-away minimizes the child's effort and control of earning while putting more control in the parents' hands. Parents often become angry and threaten to take away rewards. This sets up an unnecessary power struggle over whose self-esteem is threatened. Even though parents control what privileges are available, a rule-based model is quieter and puts the child in control of obtaining their rewards. It should be, "When you do your work, I will pay you." End of discussion. If you pay the child without their first doing

The Choose to Earn System
Figure 3

Freebees	Privileges	Jobs
Food Clothing Shelter Education Health care	Screens: TV VCR Cable Video game system Hand held video games Computer Renting video tapes Renting video games Toys and games Collections Radio/stereo CD players/Walkman Music instruments/lessons Sports teams/equipment Special clubs Bicycles New clothes Telephones Curfews: Bedtime/Go out Friends over/visit/sleep-over Private room/door Snacks/restaurants/fast food Private schools/camps Pets Trips and vacation Nice home/air conditioning Pools/beaches/movies/bowl Services: Money Cooking Taxi Cleaning Laundry	**Home** 1. Your Mess Room: bed/toys/clothes/trash In House: Den/bathroom/ playroom/kitchen/hallway Outside: yard/driveway 2. Chores Garbage/pet/ Recycle/dust/vacuum Set & clear **table** 3. Hygiene **School** Schoolwork Homework Study Be prepared Behavior **Respect** Manners Respect property of others Treat people nicely Handle anger appropriately Get things done on time Do favors

Notes: For children six and over give no more than two reminders. Younger children and those with special conditions may need help to do their jobs either directly or with a check **off** list. Your goal is for 80% compliance **on jobs**. Let the rules control. Don't argue. If problems occur, then ask the four questions: Is it the Adults? Is it the Children? Is it the System? Is it due to a lack of love/fun? Be positive!

Michael Simon, Ph.D., P.C. 1/2000

the chore/job, then why should they work for it? If I win the lottery, I might be inclined not to work at all.

Fig. 3 is a chart I use to teach the **Choose to Earn** model. There are what I call **freebies** that, by law, parents must give their children, such as food, clothing, shelter, healthcare, and education. Within these categories are minimal requirements including used clothes, school lunches for poor families, emergency room healthcare, public school through grade twelve, a place to live appropriate for the season, and no abuse. Parents are not required to love their children, but they cannot abuse them. Children are not required to have private bedrooms; in fact, a family can share one room. If this is all a parent can do, then they have done an adequate job according to the law. Everything else we do for our children by spending our money or sacrificing our time is a benefit or privilege.

Privileges are access to toys and entertainment systems, extra hobby programs, extended social events, communication devices, freedom of movement such as curfews and distance, and special services such as cooking, cleaning, laundry, and banking. The Choose to Earn model will be consistent well into the young adult ages. "Can I use the car?" "Well, did you complete your chores?" The less a parent says, the better. Just follow through without a power struggle argument — let the rule control. Why do we usually follow the laws of our country? It is to retain benefits and privileges. By following traffic laws, I retain my ability to use my car for my desires. I have earned that privilege. Breaking the law can result in not having that privilege.

I always presented the Choose to Earn model at a family meeting. I wanted everyone on the same page. No secrets! To help illustrate the difference between a freebie and a privilege, I would ask a child what would happen if they called the police and said, "My parents have not fed me for two days!"? Of course, they would send someone to check it out. If, however, they called the police and claimed, "My parents will not let me have a TV set," what would they do? They, of course, would not respond. A few more examples were sometimes needed to get the point across.

To reiterate, there are three areas in which children need to cooperate in order to earn privileges: **Home, School, and Respect**.

Home: At home, children need to learn to clean up after themselves. If parents organize their home as I mentioned in the previous section on Age of Discovery children, then it will be easier for the Age of Opinion child to comply.

Children make messes inside and outside the house, including in their bedrooms (toys, laundry, papers, trash, and linens) and the bathroom (dirty clothes, wet towels on the floor, and toileting mess — poor aim is a man's bane!). Play areas both inside and outside need to be cleaned up, including putting away sports equipment and bicycles. Home responsibility also includes doing **chores** to help the family. Parents work hard to help the family, and children need to learn to do their part. Who is cleaning the table, taking out trash, caring for the family pet, helping to collect laundry, and assisting with straightening up the living areas? I do not recommend an allowance for younger children for doing chores. They need to learn that the multitudes of privileges they already have are their rewards. Allowance is for older teens, but they will need to save and use it for things they want, such as concert tickets.

Home also means **hygiene**. Brushing teeth, bathing, and wearing clean clothes are required tasks for the Age of Opinion child.

I will address how to teach room-cleaning skills a bit later in the section "Teaching Skills to Earn Privileges: Structure."

School: The second area of compliance is School. What a child does in school actively affects earning privileges at home. The first job is to do their in-class schoolwork. Secondly, good behavior in school is required. Getting into trouble at school also means getting into trouble at home. Conversely, good behavior at school is rewarded at home by earning certain privileges. Thirdly, children are expected to do homework and prepare for exams and projects. If they studied but there was a problem with a test score, it is acceptable if a good effort was made to prepare. Parents must reward a good effort regardless of the outcome. If there is a problem with performance on a test, then they can look for answers together. Making a poor effort to be prepared and receiving a poor grade should result in not earning privileges.

Respect: The third area of responsibility is Respect. Children are required to show manners, respect each other's property, and speak kindly. They should be expected to do favors to help the family, such as bringing in the groceries from the car. Children, like all of us, will get angry at times. It is ok as long as they take their anger to a Safety Zone. Like all of us, children must learn to respect the laws of the country.

If children comply at least 80% of the time with a few helpful prompts, job lists, and no more than three verbal requests, then they can be given privileges. Compliance in fewer than all three areas — Home, School, and Respect — is not ok . For example, a child who has done their homework and chores, but then opens a fresh mouth or hits a sibling has still not completed the requirements to earn certain privileges.

Again, avoid arguments! Do not reason! Children will ask for privileges, and you can say, "Well, did you complete your jobs? When you do, see me, and I will pay you then." Do not fall for the child baiting you into a fight. If you find yourself getting angry, take a moment to go to your Safety Zone. The child can wait until you calm down to address the rule.

If children have not complied in all three areas, even with helpful reminders, then the privilege no longer exists. They will need to work to earn it back.

Remember, as adults we only get paid when we fulfill our job requirements. Poor effort leads to getting fired. I often ask children to give me four days in a row of effort to earn back privileges. Some adjustments for days of consecutive effort can be made for children with biological issues such as illness, age, and conditions such as ADHD.

Children need to make efforts to gain access to privileges. They can also be given the option to do extra chores to earn back their privileges sooner. Just doing time without effort is not enough. We value more that which we work harder to obtain. Privileges are classes of items such as all screens, all toys, or freedom of movements, such as visiting friends or going to events, and services provided by parents such as rides or laundry.

I liked to share this personal reference to help connect the point of my approach: I came from a home where getting hit was the main consequence for non-compliance. My sister and I were victims of our parents' moods. I grew up with major resentments towards my parents. Love was a bad four-letter word in my home. I have long forgiven my parents because I realized how damaged they were from the horrors they endured while growing up during the Holocaust. (Please see the section on **Forgiveness** in Volume Two.) Our childhood experiences, however, were unpleasant to say the least. The bad memories far outweighed the good feelings. I worked awfully hard not to repeat that life for my children. The effort to grow and understand was well worth it.

When my sons were eight and nine years old, they were giving us a hard time with cleaning up the mess they made in the den. I found my parenting style starting to resemble my parents' approach. I was determined not to repeat that for my kids. At first, I tried to be the good guy, but soon realized that I needed to find an effective way to discipline. My wife and I decided to stop arguing and told the children they would need to give us four days in a row to earn back their screen privileges, which included TV, computers, video-recording devices, etc. They gave us a few days of compliance with their jobs and then regressed. It took them three weeks to achieve four consecutive days of effort. We did not argue with them. When they asked for the screens, we asked calmly, "How many days has it been?" We told them to see us when they had complied for four days. I still read them stories at night, gave them positive attention throughout the day, and never withdrew love as a punishment. They learned over time that Mom and Dad stick to the rules. We were not tested very often after that. They knew what was needed to access their screens and rarely went without them. Whenever we were tested, the rule was enforced.

A word on values: I have found that parents often make a critical mistake in how they convey values to children regarding effort. Values should reflect priorities: 1) family, 2) school, and 3) recreation. I found, in problem households, that they were prioritized in the reverse order; recreational activities, such as sports, music, and other art programs, took precedence over family and school.

While I believe it is particularly important to help children discover their interests and learn how to work with others, these activities are still privileges. To enjoy these activities requires a parent to incur major financial expenses and sacrifice time. Many times, effort on behalf of Home, School, and Respect is ignored in favor of recreation. The team coach is not raising the child. It is a mistake to let practice and the game supersede consistently poor effort with Home, School, and Respect. Parents will rush a child to the event and later find the child too tired to study or do homework. Disrespect is ignored in favor of the game. When parents consistently grant privileges without the prerequisite effort, they confuse the child, teaching them to disregard the value of effort needed to earn privileges.

The rule-based model teaches responsibility, improves self-esteem, and fosters respect for the efforts others make to benefit our lives.

Active Listening and Problem Solving

The Age of Opinion child has a greater capacity for conversation and verbal expression of their feelings than the Age of Discovery child. Defusing an issue with active listening before it escalates into a tantrum can facilitate problem solving. This requires a parent to be patient and willingly uncover the real issue. People, especially children, rarely come right out and state their issue. They initially fish around or send out feelers to test the waters for possible reactions.

At times, a child may direct an emotional barrage toward an unwitting parent. For example, a child comes home from school and shouts, "I hate you, Mommy!" This should be a signal that something has upset the child. A parent who jumps all over this comment, overreacts, or applies discipline will often miss the point. They shut down the conversation and never find out the real meaning of the angry comment. Children clam up when pressed with the third-degree. In addition to poor modeling, they send a clear message to the child that they cannot trust their parent to talk with them or help in any way. Over time, a wall is erected between parent and child that could be exceedingly difficult to deconstruct.

A better approach is to use **active listening**. Try to be a mirror, reflecting the feelings you are sensing. Do not rush into problem solving. Take a long, slow breath. It can take four or five more reflections to uncover or get to the point. This is also an important skill I taught in couple therapy.

Let's review a possible dialogue of an angry child coming home from a school day:

Child: "I hate you, Mommy!"
Parent: "You seem angry at me." (Be patient and wait. The child may continue to express upset feelings toward you. Remember, adrenaline is rushing through them.)
Child: "I am really very angry at you." (Continue reflecting calmly that you hear their anger.)
Parent: "You seem so angry at me." (The child may add some new information.)
Child: "It's your fault!"
Parent: "I did something you didn't like?"
Child: "I hate school!"
Parent: "It seems you're angry about something at school."
Child: (Adrenaline rush is subsiding) "Yeah. I hate lunch."
Parent: "You're upset about lunch?"
Child: "Well, not everything — just dessert. Billy had cookies and I had fruit. I wanted a cookie and he teased me. Billy always teases me. I don't like Billy because he is mean to me."
Parent: "Ok, so let's see: you seem upset with Billy, and it seems you don't know what to do about his teasing you."
Child: "Yeah, Mom. What should I do? I'm sorry. I love you. Can you help me?"
Parent: "I love you, too. Let's do some brainstorming and problem solving."

At this point, the child has calmed down and can now be helped with the real issue of being teased. A parent overreacting to the "I hate you" comment would never get to the helping phase. Initially, a parent must accept that biology must run its course before they can get to security and problem solving.

Keep in mind that a child expressing verbal anger because of a rule being enforced is having a tantrum. Avoid the argument and still reflect: "Ok, you are angry at me." Stay with this comment until they give up. Encourage, calmly, that they need a Calm Out. Losing patience and threatening to take away privileges will only incite more rage. It is like adding fuel to the fire. Later, when the child has calmed down, you can talk about how the child could have handled the situation better. Disrespect in this situation only serves to delay earning the privilege, and effort must still be made to earn it back.

Try to listen to how words are expressed to gain the true messages. Reflecting helps to be more accurate.

Teaching Skills to Earn Privileges: Structure

All children, as well as adults, need to be trained how to do their jobs to earn their pay/privileges. Children, especially those with special needs such as ADHD, require skills to stay on task and focus on the job. Most often, children do not know where to begin a task. They have trouble "seeing the *trees* for the *forest*." This can often be an issue of biology rather than laziness.

Cleaning up a child's bedroom is a good example. For the room to be cleaned, there are many tasks to attend to, such as toys, laundry, trash, and making the bed. If a parent sends a child, particularly one with attention and impulse issues, into a room to clean up, they will often grab the first thing they find and walk out, saying, "It's clean." The parent then says, "No way. Go back and do more." The game continues, the child grabs another item and again declares, "It's clean." There is no third trip to the bedroom without a meltdown. The problem is due to a lack of structure and training.

Develop a "road map" for the whole task. For cleaning a bedroom, it is required that the child put toys away, put clothes in the hamper, throw away trash, and make the bed. (I do not hold young children accountable to dust and vacuum.) Make up a nice checklist to remind the child what they need to do for Home, School, and Respect. I have included a sample checklist. **See Fig. 4 (Page 52)**

A checklist, however, that hangs on a wall or door will soon become wallpaper that no one notices. Place the checklist on a clipboard with an attached pencil. A child can carry the clipboard with them. Do not overload the checklist; just include the basic tasks that will earn them their privileges. Having the list is helpful, but it will not be enough. Children have trouble focusing. They often do not know where to start a task and will need a direction.

Using the "road map"

Place a box for collection in the center of the room. Choose one item on the list and say, "Ok, let's pick up toys (or clothes, etc.)." Begin the path at the right or left side of the room, depending on hand preference, then have the child place their hands next to their eyes to focus direction. The hands work like blinders to keep peripheral distractions away. Choose an area about shoulder width and, with their hands to guide their focus, ask, "Are there any toys to pick up here?" Continue doing this one shoulder-width area at a time, progressing in a circle around the room until you return to the starting point. Developing a path is essential to not miss objects. A good housekeeper always develops a path to follow when cleaning up.

Daily Checklist
Figure 4

	Time	M	T	W	TH	F	S	SU
My Room								
❖ Put toys away								
❖ Put clothes away								
❖ Papers in the trash								
❖ Make my bed								
❖								
❖								
Family Chores								
❖ Pick up my things around the house								
❖ Take out the trash								
❖ Kitchen chores								
❖ Help with pets								
❖ Outside chores								
❖								
❖								
Self Care								
❖ Brush my teeth								
❖ Take my bath								
❖ Take out my clothes for tomorrow								
❖								
❖								
School								
❖ Homework								
❖ Study								
❖ Schoolwork								
❖ Behavior								
❖								
❖								

Michael Simon, Ph.D., P.C. May 2002

Once the toys are collected, check the item off the list. The next task is to put clothes away. Place the box in the center and repeat the same hand-eye coordinated path, only looking for clothes. Once collected, disperse them where they belong. Mark clothes off the checklist. Do the same routine for collecting trash. Once toys, clothes, and trash are picked up, it easier to see the bed and straighten it up.

I have instructed children with **ADHD** issues with this approach, and they could clean up a room in less than ten minutes without a meltdown. I have taught this procedure to adults with the same attention issues to improve doing their jobs at work, and for uncluttering their homes. With structure, they retained their jobs and became able to tidy their living areas.

Parents need to work with the child by modeling and, if need be, using gentle, hand over hand guidance from behind to direct them through the path. Reasoning rarely works. Practice and structure with positive reinforcement are more effective.

This same method of developing a path can be applied to play areas both inside and outside the house. If you also have chosen not to let your home get out of control by limiting the flow of toys, the child will have an easier time cleaning. If it becomes a dump, then the task will overwhelm their sensory systems, and emotional meltdowns will be more frequent.

The **oppositional personality** child will always test your willingness to be consistent. Their goal is to get the most with the least amount of effort. The Choose to Earn system, if applied firmly and consistently, holds the child accountable for earning rewards/privileges. It will eventually become the method of choice as opposed to an emotional meltdown. Sticking to the rules is essential. If parents give in to the oppositional child and let them have privileges without effort, they will be harder to bring back into control.

Schedule clean-up periods when biological needs, such as hunger, fatigue, or illness, do not interfere. Have the rewarding activity follow the clean-up.

> *Children need to be taught how to do tasks according to their biological and developmental stages.*

Homework and Study

Doing homework and studying are also required tasks to earn privileges. Parents must be willing to go through school all over again as they will need to help their child with their homework and study. When the child arrives home from school, first allow some time to unwind and account for **biology** before beginning homework.

Each child has their own unique, optimal way to work and stay focused. Parents need to adjust to the **child's individual style**. It is important to organize the child's work area. Where does your unique child work best? Is it under the table, standing at a counter, or sitting in a quiet room? The answer depends upon their unique biological learning system. Children with ADHD often need space to fidget or move about while they learn.

Open backpacks daily to keep them organized. Often, the pack can turn into a black hole where assignments and important papers have a way of vanishing. Parents may need to use color-coded folders and binders to keep materials accessible. Develop a calendar to record when tests and projects are due, as well as when to bring gym clothes on gym day. Make up a **backpack checklist** that can be fastened to the pack to help the child stay aware of what they need to take along or bring home from school. (See the sample backpack checklist in Fig. 5 below.

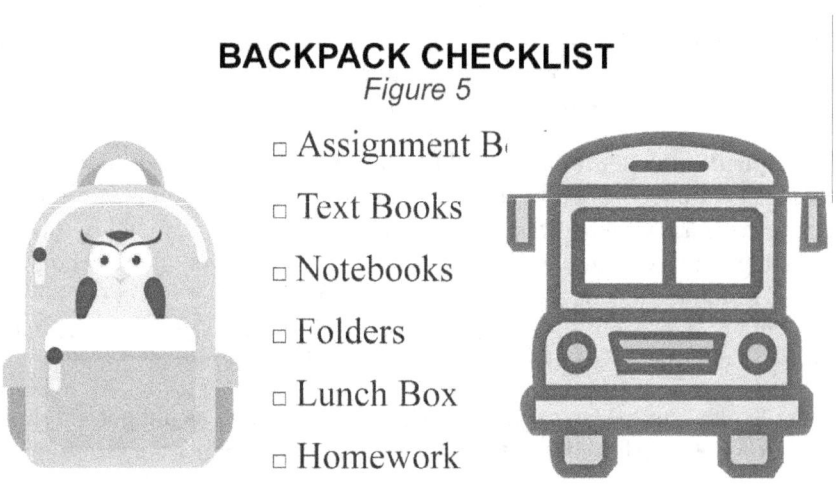

BACKPACK CHECKLIST
Figure 5

☐ Assignment B(
☐ Text Books
☐ Notebooks
☐ Folders
☐ Lunch Box
☐ Homework

In children with memory issues such as ADHD, I have often found that frustration comes with written work. As they are writing, they get distracted and can forget what they want to write. Prior to writing, have them organize ideas and then use a **recording device** to store them. As the student becomes distracted, they can listen to what they recorded to refresh their memories.

Doing homework is like taking a hike. One must **pace** themselves and stay focused on the reward at the end of the activity. One of my personal interests is hiking. As a hike leader for various clubs, it was important to me that everyone enjoyed the day and looked forward to a nice, after-hike reward of a burger and brew (B&B). Before the hike, I would prepare maps, first aid kits, and a list of materials that each hiker would need. I always scheduled the hardest part in the beginning, when the hikers were fresh. We took breaks to attend to biology — things like water and snacks — while getting through the uphill climb. I tried to keep a positive and humorous attitude to give encouragement. As the day went on, having the easier trail at the end of the hike kept our spirits up. We looked forward to the B&B, our just reward. If I had made the finish difficult, then hikers would become cranky, lose interest in doing more hikes, and be too tired to go out for the after-hike B&B.

As with homework, if a child cannot see a **path** to their just reward, such as video time, they will become frustrated and cranky, fighting you to the finish line. Take the most difficult task first and break it into smaller units. Once you have finished a segment, attend to biology: snack, stretch, and toilet. Keep up a positive attitude. As the easier tasks are saved for the end, the child can more easily stay motivated knowing they will soon have their just reward.

As always, stay out of reasoning and arguing. Remain consistent with the rule-based system. You must also model what you want your children to do. If you are messy, then children become messy. If fighting and arguments persist, then it will be important to step back to a Safety Zone to calm down.

A calmer mind thinks better!

With a calmer mind, assess the status of the four sections of the country: Are there parental problems? Are child needs and issues being addressed? Are rules fair and being enforced? Is love and attention being given? Addressing these questions will help to find answers and stop blame.

Remember to respect biology, provide smaller steps and structure, and apply earning privileges.

Stage Three: Teenage Thinkers

Now that you have your home running smoothly, a new breed of child emerges to make life more challenging. I refer to children between the ages of twelve and eighteen as Teenage Thinkers. They are remarkably like Age of Discovery children. Their needs also reflect major **biological** changes that will dominate their development. New biological issues, such as sexuality and physical appearance, will emerge. **Social** needs become extraordinarily strong as a way of self-definition.

It is important to note that the degree of their new emerging physical and sexual development can present quite a challenge for parents and teens. Adults often do not like to look back on their own turbulent adolescent years. Parents need to take a moment and recall how they felt during their awkward teen years. The issue at hand is that nature is often working in opposition to parents and societal wishes. Heightened sexual feelings are nature's way of trying to ensure the continued survival of the species.

As an example, in the Jewish religion, boys and girls turning thirteen are given a *bar* or *bat mitzvah* — a ceremony to announce that they are now considered an adult member of the community. Other religions have similar rituals. The significance of these rituals is not based purely on religious beliefs but is grounded mostly in biology. Teen years begin the physical capacity for procreation.

Thousands of years ago, societies reflected more of the natural biological cycle of survival and reproductive needs. Formal educational systems did not exist like they do today. Adolescent and even younger children often became apprentices towards skilled jobs that supported the community. They learned to be bakers, carpenters, hunters, and other vocations. People also had a much shorter life span. Culture was based on agricultural development. Ample land was available. Children often had prearranged marriages and married in their mid-teens. By age twenty, a woman may have had many babies, though often many did not survive. It was perfectly normal for reproduction to begin as a teen to ensure that an adequate number of children survived into adulthood. Those same urges to reproduce still exist today with teens. Our biological nature has not significantly changed in thousands of years.

Today's society has, for a long time, realized that we no longer need an excess of population. Food and goods are now manufactured in abundance. The cost of managing a host of teenage mothers with children is prohibitive. As nature pushes our teens sexually, society has switched messages to restrict this natural process.

Another important biological aspect to consider is brain development. We have come to understand that our brains do not fully develop until our mid-twenties. Thousands of years ago, this presented less of a concern. Life was less complex. Now, as we live much longer and function within different societal norms, it takes considerably longer for teens to grow up. Teens often insist on a world of immediacy — now or never! Unlike the baby who cries with tears, they cry with strong words. They will engage in arguments, trying to expose parents' vulnerabilities. They try extremely hard to show that they are independent and that parents do not control them.

It is in this stage that earlier parenting mistakes will come back to haunt a parent. If they have not already established a rule-based household, they will have little success trying to establish it now. It can be done but not easily. Spoiled kids will demand that the world stay as it is, giving in to their every wish.

Newly emerging social needs also place considerable distress upon teens. Self-image and confidence can fluctuate daily. Mood swings are common. The drive for social acceptance can, at times, be so compelling that any connection, whether good or bad, is better than no connection at all. An unhappy teen is very susceptible to problems with anxiety, depression, and acting-out.

It is common for teenagers to want to try out different self-expressions to define themselves. Clothing choice, hair styles, music interests, political and religious identifications, and social group connections can shift frequently. Just when you think you have figured them out, they will change preferences. Allowing some freedom of expression is healthy.

Teens who become overly invested in extremism may be sending a message that reflects more serious concerns. Parents should stop and consider the Family as a Country model and note problems at all levels that are occurring. Acting-out is often a reflection of systemic problems.

Individual and family therapy can be especially helpful. If the teen has become invested in drug and alcohol abuse, then intense rehabilitation programs may be required.

If parents have not established close, loving relationships with their kids, teens will aggressively seek out peers for approval and for values. Angry, sad, or depressed kids have a way of finding each other. They support each other's bad feelings and collectively blame their parents. "We are ok— it is all of them who are wrong." An isolated child with poor social connections is very much at risk for acting out dangerously with behaviors like drug abuse or violence, as well as withdrawing into depression. These kids would really like a closer, positive adult relationship, but they will not easily let their guard down and trust the adult world. If parents calmly persist, even when they are being verbally attacked, teens will eventually drop their defenses as long as the parent has not hurt them emotionally.

Parents should try to engage in non-threatening, age-appropriate play, such as a sport activity, theater or musical activity, cosmetic makeovers, camping, or another short trip. Finding ways to relax together can help to bring down barriers.

It's important to hang in there. Effort is still required to earn privileges. Remember to use active listening. Defuse a situation by reflecting and uncovering deeper messages. Listen to the teenager's feelings, and consider their opinions and interests. This is what we do in therapy.

The teenager is expected to take on more involved tasks, such as laundry, cooking, and routine cleaning like dusting and vacuuming. One of the best ways to teach responsibilities is to let teens face the consequences of their choices. Let us consider, for example, laundry service. Many teens love to throw clean and dirty clothes all over their rooms. They will gladly give you three loads of dirty and three loads of clean clothes to wash. Rather than rant about how they do not appreciate how hard you work to do laundry, teach the teen to do their own laundry. As it piles up in their room, avoid the temptation to do it for them or to rant about it. In time, they will take on the responsibility themselves. Necessity is the mother of invention!

Earning an allowance can be a particularly helpful tool to use with teens. An allowance will only be meaningful when they need to save and spend their own money for items like movie or concert tickets. If they are not required to use the allowance, the accumulated money loses its power to motivate. As they accumulate money for responsibility, be mindful of inflation.

Teenagers should be encouraged to find part-time, after school and weekend jobs. Earning money to use for personal purchases builds a sense of responsibility. Like an allowance, money should be earned and used to keep its value. When earning larger sums of money from a part-time job, I encourage a three-way split in how it is distributed. One third should go into long-term spending goals, such as buying a car or for college tuition, another third goes toward saving up for items like concert tickets, special clothing, or hobbies, while one third is for daily pocket spending.

The System of Love and Attention

Returning to **Figure One (Page 20)**, the **Family as a Country**, there are two foundation systems that hold up the base of the country/family. Balancing out the foundation System of Law and Order is the **System of Love and Attention**. As addressed throughout previous sections, it is once again especially important to highlight this area of need. Any form of discipline must be balanced with love and positive attention. Discipline without balance will be ineffective and creates angrier children. Attention and love without discipline will create a different set of problems with spoiled and indulged children, and will also eventually create anger.

It is particularly important that the bulk of family time is positive. A rule-based system is easier to enforce without anger. Just follow the rules. Positive time refers to playing with kids, kind conversations, praise, and unconditional love.

At night, a child needs to feel loved when going to bed. Guilt or withholding love should not be the primary method of control. Even if a child is difficult to raise, parents should still strive to find at least five sincere positive comments to make to each child daily. In addition, the power of hugs and loving touch can be felt throughout a lifetime. I regret that I cannot remember having that loving touch from my parents. I envy adults that still have that tactile memory. Fortunately, I learned to give affection to my kids.

Love and positive attention, along with fair rules and consequences, support the family/country.

Monitoring the Country (Family)

The Family as a Country must monitor four areas of need: the needs of adults, the needs of the children, consistency of the rules, and love and attention. I have been addressing these areas throughout previous sections.

When there is a breakdown in the country, cooperation is declining and emotions are rising, then it is time to call for a **family meeting**. Anyone in the family can ask for a family meeting. There are certain rules that should apply. When I lead a family meeting session, the first rule is that no one is forced to talk. Usually an adult will take the role of chairperson. Keep the meeting to no more than forty minutes.

Another important rule is to start the session without complaining or ranting. It will set a better tone if you begin by going around the room and asking everyone to say something nice to each person. For instance, "Thank you for cooking dinner," or "I like how you looked in that new outfit," or "Thanks for helping with the homework." It is amazing how members of the family are thirsting to hear a compliment. Families in trouble have stopped noticing positive behavior.

Next, put an agenda together. Ask each person to state something they are upset about. To set a better tone, parents should refrain from responding with an angry lecture or rant. The goal is to gain understanding while giving permission for a member to feel safe expressing a negative feeling. Listening and reflecting may lead to insightful information.

Once there is an agenda, select a less complex, easier item to problem solve first. Ask for suggestions and see what is possible to change. It will be impossible to tackle every agenda issue in one meeting. Make a promise to return to the agenda at the next meeting. Set a date for the next meeting and try to stick with it. Failure to keep up meetings will make it harder to communicate within the family. See if everyone can pledge to work on the issues that have been addressed. Put up a sign with a catch phrase to help everyone stay on task, such as "Did we put our shoes away today?" When there is a need for a therapeutic intervention, do not be afraid to get help. As the saying goes, beating a dead horse will not bring it to life!

An open and fair family meeting can begin to bring the family/country back together.

Childhood Therapeutic Interventions

My work with children involved **teaching** methods and skills for coping with major stresses. I will address my approaches to anger management, low frustration tolerance, handling teasing, anxiety and OCD, toileting issues, sleep problems, improving poor social skills, and family trauma, such as divorce and loss.

I have already addressed the need for parents to be involved with therapy and a plan for organizing the home/country. Working with children, parents were required to join part of the sessions near the end to review what the lesson was and go over the family's therapy homework. There was, of course, a need for confidentiality with very private feelings the children expressed, but for teaching skills the training was held jointly.

Addressing the needs of the Age of Discovery child mostly involves teaching parents how to manage their homes. These ideas have previously been addressed. Talk therapies are not very effective at this age. There are some young children, however, who can benefit by individual play therapy. These kids may be affected by major loss of security issues, such as the death of a family member, divorce, or fear generated by natural disasters, such as hurricanes or geo-political conflicts like terrorist attacks. They often cannot verbally express their anxiety. It is observed from problems with sleep, appetite, and over-emotional responses, such as sadness and anger. Young children often take their emotional cues by sensing the feelings of those in charge, i.e. the parents. How well a parent is coping will greatly affect the reactions of the children/citizens.

Therapy for these youngsters often involves the therapist joining the child's world and becoming a stabilizing security agent. Play therapy is used to give a sense of calmness and security to the anxious child. At the same time, the therapist will strive to help the parent/government regain their security role model.

The Age of Opinion child and Teenage Thinkers are children who are able to engage in instructional and talk therapy. As mentioned earlier, I strived to teach coping skills to my clients. Coping skills involve learning a healthy mindset and new behavioral skills. Many of the children I saw had issues that were also complicated by biological problems such as ADHD, OCD, or innate personality traits.

Problems with frustration tolerance and anger management, such as an inability to handle doing poorly on a test, participating in a competitive game activity, responding to teasing, or social rejection, were common in the children I worked with.

The Experience Road vs. the Failure Road

In the Introduction to this book, I presented the Experience Road vs. Failure Road approaches to life. Please refer to that section to refresh your understanding of this concept.

Treatment for anxiety, depression, and anger-management/frustration control involves a **mind-body** transformation. The mind sets the stage for the body's reaction. It is important to address both aspects when treating behavioral/psychological issues. My teaching model of therapy always began with a clear understanding of how our minds/brains work. Understanding this process will facilitate understanding of how to change beliefs, which is needed to change one's behavior.

It is especially important to understand that **we make our own feelings** based on how we think about what is happening. Information is picked up through our senses and quickly filtered through our way of thinking, then we choose a reaction behavior. This happens in the blink of an eye. If the brain perceives a threat based on our way of thinking, it sets off an emergency response system that charges us with a chemical reaction and gives us immediate energy. This is called the fight-or-flight response. Our brains will switch focus from whatever is currently on our minds to preparing for immediate danger. As an example, consider how we react to teasing. How we react to being called a name will depend upon how we have learned to interpret the words we are hearing. There can be many different interpretive reactions to the same stimulus/word. The fact is that people do not make our feelings — we make our own feelings based on how we think. Think of it this way: offense is not given, it is taken. The tease does not make us angry; it is what we tell ourselves about being teased that gets us angry. A tease begins as a sound that vibrates through the air and enters our ears. It is then filtered through our beliefs and then our body chooses a reaction response.

When we are born, we come into the world with a biological foundation but without instructions as to how the world works. At an early age, we are taught how to think by sources around us, such as parents, religions, government, social media, and the entertainment world. My goal in therapy was to teach a philosophy to life that would improve our feelings/reactions by changing how we interpret events.

We have a **choice** in how to think about the world around us. As I previously pointed out, there are **two roads of life** we can live by. I try to teach everyone to see life from the **Experience Road** not the **Failure Road**. Mindset training involves teaching how to think constructively in various situations. Parents and children are taught together to try to look at life as a place for learning experiences. I do not believe in failure. No matter the event, you can always learn something from the experience. When knowledge is acquired, the experience is a success. They key is choosing not to accept failure and/or to obsess on negative thinking.

We never fail — we only learn!
Every experience has something to teach us.
We only succeed!

Cognitive Training

My teaching children a positive mindset way of thinking, or cognitive training, began with a series of short stories, each with an important message about how to be positive when facing frustration. The book I used was written by Dr. Virginia Waters (1980). It is a group of short stories written for children that strive to teach a more constructive way to think about issues, such as accepting an imperfect world, handling teasing, coping with mistakes and disappointments, and improving self-esteem. They follow the teachings of rational emotive behavioral therapy (REBT) as developed by Dr. Albert Ellis, the founder of REBT. I had the great experience of learning at the Institute for Rational Living during the period when Dr. Ellis was alive. His ideas are well engrained in my work and personal life.

The stories are presented in a stepwise progression to teach new ways of thinking. With each short story I read with a child, I developed a sign to be taken home, posted in a prominent place, and referred to daily as a family belief or philosophy to life. It was particularly important that parents participated with this process. It was family homework!

People need to stay extremely focused on new ways of thinking or behaving in order to make changes. Creating signs is a reminder to stay aware, just like road signs on a highway help us stay aware of rules and locations. Without conscious effort to remain focused, we revert to old, less appropriate habit. See the Appendix for sample signs I used.

It was often difficult to get parents to follow through. Many times, signs were not clearly posted, and the concept was not frequently referred to at home and school. The signs were often placed in out-of-view places, such as behind a door. They were even left in the car. Just randomly hanging up a sign without reflecting on its content is not going to work. These actions represented parental resistance to change their own ways of thinking. They just wanted me to tell the child to behave, as if I had a magic wand to make this happen! Remember, reasoning will not work. Only by practicing and staying conscious of new ways of thinking can we improve our lives as well as our children's lives. Consistent effort was needed to get this point across. Frequent reinforcement to incorporate new ways of thinking was required.

The first story I would read was about a boy named Norman who was so upset about the world not being perfectly his way. Eventually, Norman meets a magician who teaches him that it is better to "make the best of it," accepting that it is ok when sometimes you do not get your way. This phrase became the first sign in triggering the family's way of thinking and responding. When events are not going your way, follow the Experience Road: see what you can learn from the experience, and make the best of it!

The second story, Maxwell's Monster, dealt with anger/frustration problems. The story illustrates the "monster thoughts" we tell ourselves that create overreactions rather than better, more constructive thoughts that help us cope with difficult situations. I created and used three major concepts to highlight this issue: **It's Not HAT: Horrible Awful Terrible; It's Only FAD: Frustrating Annoying and Disappointing; and "Monster Thoughts" vs. Better Thoughts. See Fig. 6 (Page 64) and Fig. 8 (Page 156).**

Events that are **FAD** are events that are temporary, without long-lasting, life-threatening consequences. We can easily live with a FAD event. Some examples are your favorite team losing the big game, not doing well on a test, your friend not coming over to play, etc. It is fine to feel somewhat badly, but we can more easily "make the best" of these disappointments. You can see your friend at another time, and no one dies if your favorite team loses a game.

HAT situations are those that are so bad that people can die from them. **HAT** events dramatically affect your life. Our society frequently models overreacting with HAT mentality. As an exercise, notice how often people around us express HAT when, at worst, it's only FAD!

Children can have a hard time picturing and understanding the concept of HAT and FAD without a visual reference. To teach a child how to distinguish between events that were **HAT** and **FAD,** I often asked children and parents to collect articles from the newspaper that highlighted HAT or FAD events, such

Figure 6

MONSTER THOUGHTS	BETTER THOUGHTS
It's **HAT**! Horrible, Awful, Terrible	It's **FAD**! Frustrating, Annoying, Disappointing
I **CAN'T** stand it!	I don't like it, but I **CAN** stand it.
I **MUST** get my way!	I'd like to have it, but I **DON'T HAVE** to have it.
You're a **HORRIBLE** person!	I don't like your **BEHAVIOR**.

Michael Simon, Ph.D

as delayed school openings due to weather conditions, wars, natural disasters, auto accidents, etc.

I focused on these concepts as the primary beliefs used to treat anger/frustration issues, anxiety, depression, and OCD. I also used these concepts with the adults I saw and gave out signs to them as well. "It's not HAT" and "It's only FAD" became so ingrained into my clients' thoughts, that, years later, I received letters thanking me for teaching them the concepts which they still used in their daily lives. When they felt upset, they pictured themselves taking off the "HAT" and reminding themselves it was only "FAD."

With Age of Discovery kids, I also used a series of books called *Sweet Pickles* (Perle, Reinach, & Hefter, 1977). The characters became reference points to try to alert a child when they were acting or thinking like a story character, e.g. the "Nasty Nightingale" or the "Very Worried Walrus." We made pictures from the book covers for the kids to hang up at home. These references became cues to initiate coping skills.

Whenever possible, I coordinated with teachers and shared my signs to use in the classroom. The more involved that teachers became, the better the possibility that the concept could generalize beyond the home setting. I even hung signs in my waiting room to increase awareness.

Step One of cognitive training was to establish new ways of thinking and incorporate them into the family thinking process. Step Two involved learning about **biological reactions to our thinking**. If a child or adult could interpret an event not as a catastrophe or a threat, then their body would respond with calmness, and the mind would stay in control, helping to "make the best of it."

When we interpret an event as a threat, our mind control diminishes, and it is imperative to address the biological reaction(s) first. The body's response can be used as a signal to initiate a coping response. As was mentioned earlier in the section "Restraint Techniques for Aggressive Behavior," **find a Safety Zone**. Do not forget that we get a sudden surge of adrenaline when we perceive danger, regardless of whether it is real or not. This causes our breathing to become more rapid and our muscles to tense up. The brain receives less oxygen. To conserve energy and resources, the brain/mind focuses only on the immediate, perceived danger. Often, we are pulling a **false alarm**, overreacting to a non-threatening event. The first step in anger management is to get to a Safety Zone and calm our bodies down. Sometimes, when under duress, we go forward into a danger zone and lose more control of our minds, resulting in more poor behavioral responses fueled by an increase in adrenalin reactions.

If you lose control of your thinking, you will lose control of your body. To regain control of your thinking, first get control over your body.

Anger and Frustration Control: A Four-Step Program

With anger and frustration issues, I teach children and adults a **four-step program: Stop, Step Back to a Safety Zone, Breathe, and Think**. See Fig. 7 on Page 66.

Anger Frustration Control
Figure 7

To Control Anger And Frustration; Do The 4 Steps

1. STOP Listen to your body. Don't rush into it!

2. STEP BACK TO A SAFETY ZONE Give yourself some space to work it out! Take your anger out on something that won't cause harm to a person or an object. If you have to hit something, then use a bean bag, pillow, or Nerf ball.

3. BREATHE Keep your body loose don't tense up. Take 3-5 minutes to catch your breath.

4. THINK Is it really HAT: <u>Horrible, Awful</u> and <u>Terrible</u>? I don't like it but I can stand it. Do I need to make trouble for myself? What can I do about it?

Michael Simon, Ph.D., P.C.

Step One: Stop! This involves learning to read your body. What do you feel like when you are angry, frustrated, or anxious? Be aware of body tension in your hands, feet, stomach, and chest. Note your increased heart rate, shallow breathing, and inability to focus.

Step Two: Step Back to a Safety Zone! Begin to slowly — or if need be, quickly — move away from the area. This gives you space to calm down and work it out. Time spent in a Safety Zone will depend on how quickly you can regain mind control. It could take as little as five minutes, up to an hour or more.

I once had a frantic call from a mother whose nine-year-old daughter had been lying on her bed, screaming for the better part of an hour. "I'm going to kill her," the desperate woman said. The mother needed to move to her own Safety Zone. I spoke with her for a while until her body calmed down and she could see that her daughter was doing what we were teaching her. She was in her bed Safety Zone, working out the adrenaline energy. It was taking a long time, but she was not all over the house causing greater disruption. The mother was instructed to praise the child once she ceased screaming, and to give her credit for going to a safe place.

Step Three: Breathe! I taught both children and parents to use breathing techniques to slow down respiration. Getting more oxygen to the brain is essential. We worked at releasing body tension and gaining breath control. Basic yoga skills were also introduced. First, we would shake out the tension and stretch out. Second, we placed our hands on our stomachs and felt our breathing, noting how the stomach would rise and fall. Third, we would breathe in through our noses, slowly expanding our stomachs like a balloon. Keeping our bodies loose, we would hold our breath for a count of seven and then slowly exhale. I used the comparisons of smelling roses and blowing out candles.

I explained to kids that athletes do this when in a stressful situation. A pitcher on a mound steps away, loosens up, and catches his breath. A batter does the same at home plate. All successful athletes learn to control their breathing and relax their muscles. Actors also work on slow, calming breaths to keep their minds sharp before the curtain goes up. This helps them not to forget their lines.

Step Four: Think! Once the body calms down, the brain receives more oxygen and can think better. We can now engage in problem solving. We can ask ourselves, "is it HAT? Do I need to make trouble for myself or others? What can I do about it?" I facilitated role-play to practice better responses.

I also used hypnotic visualization with this process. We identified **trigger** situations that the child could not handle well, such as losing a game or being teased. While in a deep, relaxed state, I gave the child a script of being in a stressful situation, allowing them to feel their body tighten before doing the four steps, ending with a good, self-rewarding feeling. In addition, I made recordings of these scenarios to follow and practice at home.

Remember to teach skills for handling anger and frustration.

How to Manage Teasing

One of the most common problems I confronted in teaching frustration tolerance involved handling teasing. The children I saw seemed to have personalities that were vulnerable and sensitive to taunting and rejection from peers.

Many children, and especially special-needs children, have a particularly difficult time handling teasing. Some children cannot understand the nuance of a tease. Their minds are too literal, and they overreact. Their interpretations usually lead them to feel rejected.

What is a tease, actually? As previously pointed out, a tease begins as a sound that vibrates through the air and enters our ears. The vibration is sent to the brain through our sense of hearing. It is then filtered through our beliefs, and the brain chooses a reaction response. The tease has no power over us unless we think it does. Our reaction will depend upon how we have learned to interpret the words we are hearing. There can be many different interpretive reactions to the same word. Again, I emphasize that other people do not make our feelings; we make our own feelings based on how we think. The tease does not make us angry, rather it is what we tell ourselves about being teased that makes us angry.

Teasing has been around since the beginning of time. Children often use teasing as a way of testing each other. If you can handle teasing, your social status gains; but if you cannot handle teasing, you become a target for bullying and rejection. While teasing seems to be more of a verbal attack, bullying can often be a physical and intense, prolonged emotional attack. There is social competition, and children will manipulate a more sensitive child to climb the social ladder. Kids are very quick to notice any differences among their peers. Whether someone is short, tall, heavy, unathletic, bright, has an odd name, or whatever, some child will try to exploit that difference. Some children think it is funny to tease. For others, it is a way of acting out their own personal, emotional problems. Some children tease because it is modeled at home or from other prominent, public figures. The kids I saw suffered from **low tease tolerance**. Virginia Waters (1980) has a great short story about a young girl who is allergic to teasing. I usually began with that story when focusing on how to handle teasing.

As I mentioned before, my first lessons were about "making the best of it" and "monster thoughts." It was important that children understood how thinking makes our feelings. I then challenged children to try to make me angry by teasing me. I would bet $100 that they could not do it, placing one hundred dollars in front of them. Some of the children would call me everything under the sun. Yet, try as they might, I would not get angry. I pointed out that I had a choice of how I thought about the names they called me and the words they used. It was my way of thinking that made the difference between us. Calling me something didn't make me "become" that something.

Kids who could handle teasing projected self-confidence. They were proud of their unique ability. These children were quick to think up a coping thought, verbal expression, or body language that said, "I do not care what you call me." Confident kids do not care much if not everyone is their friend. They can be their own best friend.

Most kids I saw desperately wanted everyone to like them. They were too sensitive. They believed they must be perfect and rejected themselves for making mistakes. They were not born with a confident nature. Many of my clients also had biological issues, like ADHD and autism, that interfered with their ability to process information.

Desensitizing them to teasing involved the **barb** technique. Together, we constructed a list of **comebacks** to use when someone teased them — comments like, "Yeah, right, whatever," "Put it on the news," "Thanks for the compliment," "Super," "Awesome," "Like I really care," etc. Quick, sarcastic comments, when uttered with confidence, can deflect teasing. It was important to teach these children about sarcasm as a tool of using humor to show confidence. These kids had a particularly difficult time grasping the concept of sarcasm, as their thinking was often so literal.

Comebacks also serve as reminders that our first thought is especially important. The humor in our comebacks is an attempt to break the cycle of the negative thinking process of accepting the put-down. It is crucial to teach that, no matter what we say in response to a tease, we really cannot stop someone from teasing us. There is only one guaranteed way to stop someone from teasing us. I would challenge the children to try to think of a way to absolutely stop a teaser. I would ask, "Can I still tease you if you told on me, hit me, called me another name, ignored me, or paid me not to tease you?" The answer was yes, I could still tease you. "If, however, you killed me — could I tease you?" That was obviously the only way to absolutely stop me from teasing you. Killing someone, however, is definitely HAT and, of course, something we should never do!

If someone continues to tease us, we could also accept not liking that person or needing their friendship. Bullies do not care if you tell them that their teases hurt your feelings; it only fuels their effort to tease you more.

> ***Remember: words cannot really hurt you.***
> ***It is how you think about them that counts most!***

After drawing up a list of comebacks, we would decide on the top ten comments the child could use. The list varied for each child. Then, we would practice. I gave them the barb or tease and they followed up with a comeback. We used role-playing and role-modeling. Parents were also instructed to practice daily with their child at home. They were given a handout to instruct them on how to teach comebacks.

See the handout "Skill Drill: Handling Teasing" in the Appendix. Page 160.

Initially, we would tell the child we were practicing teasing drills. As time progressed, we would do **sneak attacks**. A sneak attack is a barb given without warning. Parents and children could sneak attack each other. They also could sneak attack me and try to win the $100. At home or in my group therapy sessions, children earned tokens for successful responses to sneak attacks that could be saved up and exchanged for rewards.

Body language and tone of voice are skills that have to be shaped up in response to teasing. Overreacting, such as crying or silently withdrawing, will mark a child as a target. Telling them to just ignore the teaser does not usually work; their body language of rejection betrays them. Having the right mindset, an appropriate comeback, and the right body language sends a message of confidence to other kids. Again, emphasize that not everyone will like each other or be friends: **It's Not HAT!**

Practicing how to become insensitive to teasing is better than just telling your children to ignore the tease.

Assertion and Positive Training

I would often teach a child to verbally confront a negative comment or action from another child as a first step to de-escalating a conflict. Children who are skilled bullies are very good at finding an opportunity to instigate trouble, especially when a teacher or another adult is not watching. The weaker child or target, often overreacts and draws the attention of the adult while the bully is calmly sitting back, claiming innocence as the target child gets disciplined for overreacting.

I teach children to make an **assertive** comment like, "Why did you do that?" They are taught to calmly and firmly, and with a raised voice, ask the instigator to explain themselves. If done quickly, without hysterics, an adult will turn their attention to the situation and perhaps catch the bully in action. **See Skill Drill: Why Did You Do That? On Page 169.**

Commonly, many of the kids I saw had a major problem of misperceiving the intentions of others. Asking first, "Why did you do that?" can also serve to clarify an act before overreacting. Another child could have accidentally bumped into them and could apologize without escalating a conflict.

Role-playing and modeling situations, along with sneak attack practice, are essential. New behaviors can only be established by consistent practice. Simply telling a child what to do will never work!

Assertion training also involves learning to express your ideas and feelings. It is important to be able to offer your opinion, for instance of what game to play. It is also important to learn to feel confident when going into a store or restaurant and being able to ask for assistance. Learning to have an opinion or express what you enjoy or are interested in demonstrates confidence. Making up an attractive **My Interest Chart** is a good project for children and parents. The list can include favorite games, TV shows, books, jokes, foods, places, people, etc., and can be added to or amended if an interest changes. Keep the list displayed in the child's room and hang up pictures that reflect the interests. Having pictures can help kids stay aware of their own unique selves.

Parents need to help their children enjoy and accept their own interests. Children gain confidence in their own unique interests if parents pay attention to them. Play with your kids. Remember, not all children play the same way the parent likes to play. Trying to get into your child's world is essential, especially when it is not your interest, e.g. when a child prefers science and you prefer sports. It is also important that children learn to accept that other children may not share the same interests. If they don't, it's **not HAT!**

Assertion also means learning how to verbally express your bad feelings. As addressed earlier in the section on **active listening**, parents may have to calm the child down and get control of the adrenaline reaction in order to draw out the conflicted emotion. Once the emotion is identified, use role-playing and modeling to teach how to more calmly express these feelings.

Many of the children and families I worked with were incredibly good at being negative. They would quickly find fault, overly notice only what may be incorrect, express mostly negative opinions, complain frequently, and were very demanding or aggressive. They were very weak at giving praise and positive reinforcement and required **positive training**.

During my sessions with children, either individually, family, or group, I would start with **positive drills.** Learning to give compliments was a good place to begin. Children or parents were asked to find something nice to say about each other, such as "I like your shirt." They could also tell someone they did something nice, as in "Thanks for giving me a turn," or for "helping me with my homework," etc. Parents were instructed to find five positive statements to say each day to their children. Hugs and kisses were required for younger kids. **See Skill Drill: Being Positive on Page 162**:

Another finding-positives drill I used many times was to take an object from the trash and challenge the child/family to find between ten and twenty positive comments to make regarding the object. For example, try taking a used paper cup and seeing something good or useful about it rather than seeing it as just junk. Daily practice and role-modeling are again more effective than just telling the child to be nice.

Role-playing conversation drills are also an effective way to encourage assertion and positivism. Choose a topic from the child's interest list, such as their favorite baseball team, and have a five- to ten-minute conversation on the topic. Remember to emphasize positive, emotional expression by saying things like, "That's so cool." Keep the emotion consistent with the compliment. If the child's interests are different from the parent's, then the parent should remember to work hard to learn about the child's interests.

Ignoring their interests will be misinterpreted as parental rejection. This feeling of rejection can lead to self-esteem issues.

Helping children to break out of an **emotionally constricted personality** is also important. Severely inhibited, shy, withdrawn children can become targets for bullying and develop anxiety and depression. Keep in mind not everyone is similar in nature. It is ok to be a happy, quiet person who enjoys a smaller crowd or quieter activity, just as it is fine to be a happy, outgoing, gregarious type who thrives on activity. The extremely inhibited child, however, is more likely to be an unhappy child. This can be the result of a severe emotional trauma, such as abuse or the death of a love one or friend, or an inhibited, inborn personality that does not process emotional information well. Careful assessment of the Family as a Country is necessary to rule out the factors in play. My objective with these children was to help them feel comfortable with releasing inhibitions and/or trauma.

Play therapy is immensely helpful for the **traumatized** child. The goal is to help them connect to another good source for a security parent/adult. Gaining trust in others is essential. Children who had experienced trauma presented some of the most challenging and rewarding experiences I had as a therapist. The bond I established was tested at every moment. The emotional pull upon me was extraordinarily strong. There was always a fear of self-destructive acting-out. It was important to work closely with a psychiatrist when medication was needed. At times, in-patient hospitalization was needed as well. I even faced the conflict of alerting law enforcement agencies, such as Child Protective Services. There were, of course, laws I had to follow. I also had a personal rule for when to call CPS or seek hospitalization. Simply put, if I could not sleep because I was worried about a child's safety, then I opted for additional help.

Cognitive behavioral therapy was helpful when the traumatized child was stable and able to focus. Learning how to read the body's tension was used to cue coping responses. Sensory overload was often self-generated by fears based on false expectations and misinterpretations, blocking off reasoning skills. Basic survival instincts often took over, activating the fight-or-flight response, and severe emotional overreactions would occur. These kids often spent many years in therapy and would need support systems later in life as well.

A **sensory/biological** personality issue requires teaching children how to interpret incoming sensory information. One of my first steps, particularly with young children, was reading silly stories that involved a certain emotion. I loved reading the *Sweet Pickles* (Perle et al., 1977) books and laughing with the child over the silly characters in the stories.

The more mature Age of Opinion child or Teenage Thinkers were, at times, extremely uncomfortable in situations that did not have rigid structure. They needed this structure to judge or predict their behavioral responses. Spontaneity or flexible thinking was anxiety-provoking. Desensitization and reducing inhibitions often involved playing word games.

I often began with a somewhat structured, basic word-association game, moving to random words as they developed. Then we progressed to less structured, nonsense words, such as "bebo," "neta," or "gekagoo." We would go back and forth as the child became more comfortable talking nonsense gibberish. From a developmental personality perspective, our expressive language began with nonsense gibberish. The next stage involved nonsense conversations with emotional tones to express meanings. We would pretend to be from a foreign country or outer space and talk in gibberish, expressing a feeling message from verbal gestures and tone.

At times we would try to guess the emotional meaning behind the gibberish. "Can you tell what I am feeling? *Ugh ma chu cha! Ugh ma chu cha!*" As comfort levels improved, we would practice this in group sessions or as a family. Sometimes the child and I left the office and walked around the building, talking gibberish as people passed by, as if we were two people speaking a foreign language.

Silly acting drills were also used to develop skills. Improvisation was helpful. I would take a random item in the office, such as my desk name plate, and we would act out, without sounds, what this item could be if used in another way. We would duel until we ran out of possibilities.

Another favorite silly acting drill was to take an object and bring it to life. I called this animism. What would the object say and feel if it could talk? Try being an apple feeling a worm eating it from the inside, or a light bulb that was left on too long, or a baseball being pitched and hit, or, my favorite, a tissue in a box discovering its purpose in life. We would challenge each other to be spontaneous and act out a request made by the other. No prep — just go with it. At other times we would play "Charades for Dummies," which was quick and easy.

Letting go of boundaries and improvising games led us to office balloon volleyball, baseball with rolled up paper and using hands for bats, or the "Silly Olympics." In group therapy, teens loved to play out scenes from the *Whose Line Is It Anyway?* television show, or characters and events in history. Trivia games, combined with basketball or darts, were ways of bringing divergent interests together.

Learning to express oneself comfortably develops self-confidence, social growth, and positive self-interest. *Ig nee papo ig ma!*

Treating Anxiety: Phobias and OCD

I have worked with children who had phobias, fears, post-traumatic stress, as well as obsessive-compulsive disorder. Each of these problems is related to managing anxiety. It is important to teach children the connection between our thoughts and our body reactions. A misperception sets off the fight-or-flight adrenaline response. Thoughts get stuck in a **loop** cycle, and the body continues to pump more adrenaline until it becomes exhausted. The mind's ability to regain control diminishes as time in the loop continues. It is important to learn to read the body's initial adrenaline reactions and regain control of breathing. Do not forget to step back to a Safety Zone. Once that is accomplished, then you can switch to a more appropriate set of thoughts that will short-circuit the loop.

Anxiety Loop: Initial threatening thought or interpretation > increased adrenaline > increased negative thoughts > increased feelings of anxiety and fearful and avoidant behavior.

Phobias

Some of the more common phobias I worked on were fears of bees, dogs, nighttime, traveling in cars, bad weather, getting sick, and school phobias. With each anxiety condition, I would begin with cognitive training, as explained before. I used stories and posted signs to teach that thinking is the beginning of making feelings and deciding how to behave.

As mentioned previously, it is important to teach kids early in life how our brains work. Information comes into our senses. It is interpreted in our minds, and choices are made. This entire process all happens in the blink of an eye. Remember, we are born with biological hardware strengths and weaknesses, but we have few, if any, instructions or programs concerning what to do with this information. How to think and understand our world needs to be learned. Our attitudes, beliefs, opinions, and points of view are taught by parents directly or through modeling, or by society through peers, media, and religions. Certain familial viewpoints seem to pass through families across generations.

Our brain process is like a computer. The computer has hardware but will not do much without programs being installed. It is important to teach children the programs that can help them cope with life events, while also trying to correct hardware sensory deficits where possible.

In order to access your programs and maximize coping skills, it is especially important to be able to retain control over your bodily reactions. Again— if you lose control over your body, you will lose control of your thinking. I taught breathing and relaxation skills to young children. I used much of what

I had learned from yoga and relaxation training. I taught children to identify their body tensing up and quickly start using deep-breathing skills. Slower and deeper breathing keeps our oxygen levels steady and our brain's ability to think rationally in control.

Another method I used to institute the relaxation response was to teach a child to focus on a **comforting image** that reminded them of times when they had incredibly happy feelings, such as holding their pets or a fun vacation. Children were taught to create a **buzz word** that would elicit the comforting image. When they felt tension, saying the buzz word brought up the image while at the same time starting the slow, deep-breathing process. We made recordings that were used for practice at home and updated at each new step in the process. We also created reward charts for practice.

My personal buzz word is "Tennessee." If I feel anxious, I say, "Tennessee," and a picture of hiking in the Great Smoky Mountains pops into my mind while I take a deep breath. Other times, I use "Bermuda," or "lakes." Each is a personal memory. Some of the buzz words used by my clients were "guitar," "Utah," "white owl," "biking," "puppies," and many others. These words would elicit a scene that was personal and could be used to distract the person from negative thoughts.

To establish these basic skills, parents and children were taught together in sessions and given weekly homework practice assignments. Considerable practice was needed. Parents needed to model the skills I was teaching their child. Again, just telling the child not to be afraid did not decondition an anxiety response. I had no magic words. When parents would not work as a co-therapist with me, progress was extremely limited.

Coping Response: Buzz word > Comforting Image >
Breathing and Muscle Relaxation

The next stage involves constructing a series of **hierarchical** approximation steps. They begin from a safe, calm distance and continue with gradually increasing steps that gain closeness toward the feared object. This is called systematic desensitization and shaping. Relaxation skills are applied throughout the progression, beginning at the first step, which is least frightening. As a child gains confidence in that step, they progress to the next step, getting closer and closer to the feared object.

My work on **bee phobias** highlights this process. Bee phobias are quite common with children. A bee is busy looking for flowers to collect nectar. They fly around, checking for scents that distinguish flowers from non-flowers. They fly past us, take a whiff, and determine we are not a flower. They will move on. Bees only sting when they perceive they are under attack. As a child starts flailing away, the bee reacts to what it thinks is an attack and stings.

Running away screaming becomes a conditioned response, often modeled by a parent doing the same thing.

I started the desensitization process with books written for children that teach how important bees are to our lives. We learned to **relabel** bees as good, not evil. While reading positive bee information, I was also teaching the positive-thinking and deep-breathing skills mentioned earlier. Pictures of bees that reflect their beauty were hung up at home. We even drew pictures of bees collecting pollen.

The next stage involved using visualization of a comforting image, such as holding their pet, while also visualizing a threatening situation. A series of steps were generated to gradually approach the target behavior. With respect to bees, the goal was to be able to stay outside in the garden while bees were about.

It was important to have real-life experiences with bees. Imagination will help start a coping response, but real-life experience is needed to practice the coping response. I would use my home garden as our workshop. Following learning skills, we would venture outside. I would find a safe distance where a child could control their breathing and their mind, such as sitting in the driveway, removed from any flowers or bushes. We would take a fun board game with us and play while staying in this safe place, practicing calm breathing. If a bee flew by, I would trigger their buzz word and cue in the breathing response. In ten minutes, we would move five feet deeper into the garden. Within a forty-five-minute session, I would strive to progress three segments of five feet. Each new session would start where we left off. In a few weeks, we would get to the point of standing in front of a flower and watching the bees do their tasks. Children were also taught this mantra: "If you see a bee, be still."

Parents were taught the same skills and asked to model the coping skills while practicing with their kids. It was always so important to remind parents that shaming and guilting a child who showed fear would only serve to further discourage the child from trying to face their fears. Punishment and reasoning were also ineffective and destructive. This model has been used for other insects as well. Variations were applied to other phobias like weather, dogs, school phobias, heights, and even fear of bubbles.

Obsessive-Compulsive Disorder

Working with obsessive-compulsive disorder requires a deeper understanding of how our body works. **OCD is a biological disorder**. It is not a psychological disorder. The body has a problem with neural transmission. This is not a disorder than can be reasoned away. It is no different than a person born with a physical disability. I was born to need glasses early in life. You cannot reward or punish me to see better without my glasses.

Many young children go through periods of being fixated on an object, such as a superhero, song, or toy. A child without OCD can more easily move on to another task by letting go of the object or thought. As they grow up, they obsess far less. A child with OCD cannot easily let go and move on. They develop thoughts and behaviors, such as hand washing, touching objects, or repeating phrases, that become fixed into their daily habits. Reasoning and telling a child to stop does not work. Many parents I worked with would allow the odd behavior to dominate the child's world rather than deal with the child's emotional overreaction by taking away the object or deflecting the child's attention. Over the years, these exaggerated behaviors become stuck. They defy reasoning and logic. The child becomes afraid that not doing the repetition will lead to a disaster. Something HAT will happen!

To further understand the biological aspects of OCD, let us consider **The Gatekeeper** model. Picture a tall office building with many floors of people working, while the boss's office is at the top level. Sometime during the day, an employee gets an idea they wish to share with the boss. They run down the hallway, take the elevator to the top floor, and rush towards the boss's office. Just as they are about to burst into the boss's office, a gatekeeper or executive assistant pops out and says, "STOP!" The job of this gatekeeper assistant is to **filter** incoming information and determine if it is important enough to immediately let through. If it is important, then the boss will address it right away and make an immediate executive decision. If it is not crucial, the assistant takes the information and says, "I'll take care of it, don't worry." It is the gatekeeper's job to **regulate** the flow of information being processed to keep the boss focused on the most important aspects of the business.

This process goes on all day long, repeatedly, 24/7. Without a gatekeeper, the boss's desk would get flooded with trivial information causing the boss to constantly overreact. Once the information is placed on the boss's desk, it must be immediately addressed. Sometimes, however, the gatekeeper assistant is not working. The assistant is out to lunch, on vacation, or has called in sick. The gate is left open. There is no censor. The office management breaks down and the flow of information, no matter how trivial, gets through to the boss. This is a real nightmare, an out-of-control boss.

This concept of a gatekeeper is how our human body's nervous system works as well. Information is coming through our senses all day long, even when we are sleeping. It is flowing up to the brain, our boss. Along the way there are gatekeeper sensors that determine how important that information is and then pass it up the chain as necessary. For example, as I am writing, my body is monitoring urine levels in my bladder. Currently, my brain is not directly paying attention to urine levels. I do not have the urge to use the bathroom. As levels build, up my gatekeepers will eventually get my boss's attention and determine my need to urinate. Going to the bathroom will become an important task. My boss will determine it is more important than anything else.

It is a breakdown with The Gatekeeper system that is the problem with OCD. The gatekeepers are not automatically working. I would teach children and adults to understand this and to manually install a gatekeeper. Great effort must be made to quickly identify a gatekeeper failure and to react appropriately. "Oops! I am doing it again! Let me become the gatekeeper." With training and this understanding, I found that kids and adults can gain the ability to get control and initiate a coping response, such as deep breathing, thus moving away from the need to turn the lights on and off a million times or from washing hands until they bleed. They can move on to a more important idea or task — it's not HAT!

It is important to note that we are not born blank. Our nervous systems come preprogrammed to identify certain conditions as dangerous or necessary for our survival. Babies cry to be fed, or cry at loud noises to bring attention to a possible danger. These programs are **encoded** on each nerve cell's engram or memory. Nerve cells receive a signal, analyze it, then send it along, passing though gatekeepers. If it is potentially life threatening, it is sent quickly to the brain/boss. Many messages sent through our nervous system do not require an immediate response.

Early childhood trauma can also leave an impression on a nerve cell's engram that can signal danger. This impression or message of danger can become stuck in the engram long after the events have passed. A person with OCD continues to remain fixated on a fear or obsession even in the face of no immediate danger. The gatekeeper reads the false danger signal and passes the message to the boss.

To highlight this process, imagine you have just purchased an expensive new shirt. On your first night out, you get a spot on the shirt while having dinner. This is a nice shirt, it feels so good, but now it has a spot. Some shirts can repel a stain or can be cleaned to remove the stain. There are, unfortunately, some stains that cannot be removed. Try as you might, it will live forever on the shirt. My closet is full of such shirts. So, do you throw the shirt out, cry obsessively, or continue washing it endlessly? Or do you find a way to cope with the stain? A person with OCD will obsess about the stain endlessly. A healthier coping response is to accept it has happened and try to wear the shirt under a sweater or use it more casually.

Understanding that you have a **neural stain** (no pun intended) does not bring immediate release from the stain's control; however, insight can serve to trigger better coping responses, diminishing the stain's control over you. Having this understanding, I have found, releases the patient from an endless bombardment of guilt and depression or self-degrading thoughts. It is a neurological problem, not a failure of you as a person. Even in extreme situations, similar to someone born blind or missing a limb, a person with OCD can still develop positive self-esteem and make the most of their life.

With all these new skills and understanding, a **compulsive** child must then be taught to step away from the target of their compulsion. The target has an extraordinarily strong, conditioned approach-control over the behavior. The closer they are to the target, the stronger the desire to conduct the ritualistic behavior. Moving back from the target presents a weakened attraction/ approach gradient, providing space and time to install a gatekeeper coping response.

To highlight this, let us consider a case of a child who feels compelled to check a light switch or window lock by touching it over and over beyond reasonable checking. The closer a person is to the switch or lock, the stronger the desire to do the ritual repetitive behavior. Moving away from the switch or lock diminishes the desire to go back and repeat the inappropriate behavior. While moving backwards, breathing control and thought-distraction skills are implemented with the awareness that stepping back is a gatekeeper response. Practice, with supervision, is especially important.

It is quite easy to regress to the inappropriate behavior if the moving-away response has not been strongly conditioned. Parents need to work frequently and consistently to strengthen the avoidance gradient of the child's behavior. Many children have multiple repetitive, compulsive behaviors. It will be necessary to work on only one or two at a time.

With compulsive rituals, such as handwashing or showering too long, I have used timers and clocks to help the child work towards beating the clock. If the alarm goes off, the water goes off. Rewards for beating the clock are set up as well.

Children with OCD are more susceptible to family discord. Under higher levels of stress, the body's ability to process information starts to diminish due to the fight-or-flight adrenaline response. Working to reduce stress throughout the Family as a Country is important as children will become anxious out of a fear of losing security.

In summation, reasoning will not stop an OCD behavior or overcome a phobia. It will take effort to learn and continue to practice coping skills. Parents must work as co-therapists to help their child. There are no magic words or magic pills to make this easier.

Learn to recognize when a gatekeeper is malfunctioning, accept it, and use coping skills to regain control.

Toileting Issues

One of the messier problems I have worked on is **toileting issues**. There were always a few children each year who resisted toilet training and preferred soiling their underwear or diapers. These children were of ages where they should have been easily trained. Resistance to toilet training often reflects innate stubborn and oppositional personalities. At times, toileting issues can also reflect trauma. This needs to be carefully ruled out, especially if the child has been previously toilet trained.

With the Age of Discovery child, I often used a reward program to shape new behavior. A reward is only effective if the child truly desires the reward. Young children are innately attracted to primary rewards, such as sweets. To increase the rewarding power of a sweet, it was necessary to place the child on sweet deprivation for a two-week period. During this time, the child was restricted from any sweets, such as juices, candies, cereals, ice cream, etc. After two weeks, they were craving sweets.

A large jar, which was under parental control, was placed in the bathroom. The child was instructed that, with every effort to use the toilet, a treat would be placed in the jar. When they succeeded using the toilet, they could take out a small treat. It was important that the child remained in sweet-deprivation status. The only sweets they received came after proper toileting activities. Any deviation from this process resulted in the child regressing and becoming more stubborn.

Diapers, if not age appropriate, were no longer available to wear. Should an accident happen, it was critical the parent not overreact with scolding or removing treats. The parent was instructed to stay calm, give praise for trying, and never remove love. Within a few weeks, the child would earn treats or rewards for using the bathroom away from home as well.

With older, Age of Opinion children, I often used an over-correction program to increase motivation to stop inappropriate behavior. Over-correction involves trying to totally correct the situation and more. Often, I found that the stubborn child would have an accident and either give the parent the soiled clothes or (more often) attempt to hide the clothes. It was the parent who cleaned up the mess.

With over-correction, it is the child who must clean up the mess. This involves washing and scrubbing the dirty clothes, showering, and scrubbing clean any area involved with the accident, such as bathrooms, floors, etc. They need to work extra hard to correct the behavior. The child needs to experience how much effort is required to take care of their problem. Lecturing, shaming, and guilting will not work. It is more effective to have the child experience the unpleasantness of cleaning up their own mess. Withholding privileges, such as screen time or special activities, can be used to encourage the over-correction clean-up. "When you have finished cleaning up, then you have earned your privileges." As always, it is important to stay calm and refrain from scolding or hitting the child. We do not want to make having an accident a weapon the child uses to punish the parent. A child, when angry, will often get back at a parent by doing something they know is very upsetting to that parent.

Sleep Problems

Another serious problem I ran into involved children who had developed sleep issues, such as not wanting to go to bed, trouble falling asleep, or waking up during the night. These issues were seen more often with the late Age of Discovery child and the early stages of the Age of Opinion child. As frequently mentioned, before doing any intervention, it is important to conduct a thorough assessment of the Family as a Country. Sleep problems can be a reaction to family problems. There is often a link between the parents' problems and the child's own resistance to proper sleep behavior. Many times, I found these problems to be concurrent in children with anxious or stubborn personality types.

Some children can become fixed into sleeping in their parents' bed. A young child can become frightened by severe environmental dangers, such as weather conditions, or a trauma that has occurred within the family, such as divorce. Their sense of security has been challenged. Parents may continue to let the child stay with them even after the danger has passed, believing they are giving comfort. It's also easier than struggling to get them into their own sleep space. For the sake of their own need of sleep, the parent gives in. This is a short-sighted vision. When you give in to a problem, you only delay the inevitable confrontation. The longer the delay in confronting the issue, the stronger the child's emotional resistance to change becomes. I have encountered children as old as twelve still in their parents' beds. As the child ages, they soon realize that they can use pity or sympathy as an extraordinarily strong manipulation tool against parents.

Some parents may also project their own unresolved insecurities and allow the child to stay in their bed. They use the child to comfort themselves. They are afraid of the child's temporary anger or rejection, which may reflect the parents' own childhood security issues. I have also found this quite common with spousal issues. Some parents replace their spouse with the child rather than deal with relationship conflicts. This is a profoundly serious problem! Remember, it is particularly important to treat *all* members of the country/family.

In treating this problem, I helped parents to understand the importance of a child sleeping in their own space. A child needs to gain confidence in their own ability to keep themselves safe and be able to comfort themselves. When parents overreact, letting the child stay in their bed, it sends a message to the child that there is possibly a danger that requires parental protection. When a parent is confident and calmly firm while keeping the child in his or her own bed, it sends a message that all is safe. A child who wakes up in their own bed develops self-confidence that they are safe and capable of comforting themselves. Fostering insecurities well beyond the early years often results in a socially awkward, insecure child/teenager/adult.

Parents need to avoid sleeping in the child's bed. This is also a common mistake. It still sends a message to the child that it is not safe to sleep alone. Inappropriate parent-child attachments may occur and persist further, confusing a child's psycho-sexual development. Children need to become comfortable with their own selves and in their own space. They need a degree of privacy to explore thoughts and their own bodies. With new insights, the parents need to be firm but not threatening when putting their child to bed.

If the parents are not the cause of sleep problems, there may be other factors interfering with getting a child to go to sleep which are still the responsibility of the parents. The parent should always think **biology first** when a child is showing resistance. It is possible that a child maybe hungry, ill, or over-tired. Bedtimes should reflect a consistent time schedule. The body gets used to a rhythm or cycle. Getting up in the morning should also be consistent. What a child has eaten can affect sleep. Having meals too close to bedtime or eating too many sugary foods or snacks will not help settle the child's biology. A child's biology can also be upset by too much sensory stimulation. Hours playing video games or watching TV just before bed can over-stimulate their brains. This will wake them up. Intense exercise too close to bedtime can also increase adrenaline levels and delay the onset of sleepy feelings.

Some children have problems with the comfort of the sleep area. Children with ADHD have trouble filtering out discrete sounds from the foreground and background. All the sounds around them blend. Each separate little sound is as strong as any other. Sounds of people talking, walking around the house, opening the fridge, TV, showering, and street noises can keep them awake. Finding one kind of steady masking sound can help. Many children can be soothed by a certain sound. It may be ocean sounds, melodic drums, white noise, or even Tibetan monks chanting. It will depend on the child and will require experimenting with various sounds. Some children even do well with ear plugs or sound reduction headsets.

Some children will struggle to calm their muscles down. They can be hyper to a degree and will fidget uncomfortably. With these kids, a comforting bath before bed may help. A short massage can also help at bedtime. Temperature and the amount of light in the child's bedroom are also important factors. We are programmed to fall asleep with cooler temperatures and darkness. A child might like a small nightlight, but dim the overall light. The general comfort level of the bed is another important factor that can be adjusted.

Parents can help to induce sleep by having a comforting ritual: reading a happy story, songs, or prayer. Keep biology consistent: washing up, brushing teeth, toileting, then a comfort ritual with brief snuggles, hugs, kisses, and "I love you." All of this occurs in the child's room and bed. These activities are set up to become a trigger mechanism to signal relaxation and let sleep occur. I, myself, need a few minutes of reading at bedtime to clear my mind and bring on sleep. Do not read the phone or tablet as the light can stimulate the brain.

Yet another group of kids delays sleep to gain more attention from their parents. Parents need to observe what kinds of attention their children are getting during the waking periods of the day. Remember, conflicts at home within the family/country can manifest as sleep problems. Parents fighting, yelling, or uttering threats of punishment at bedtime will induce the fight-or-flight adrenaline response, further delaying the onset of sleep.

After controlling biology and external and emotional factors, the anxious child may still require therapeutic intervention to learn how to control anxious feelings. I used cognitive training and behavioral skills, such as relaxation training. Children were taught to stop catastrophizing thoughts and to control their breathing. I used hypnotic imagery to teach children to find their comforting images and even follow self-relaxation programs.

When the anxious child awakens during the night, the parent needs to get the child back into bed. Check biology and then remind the child to use the coping skills you have been practicing at home. Take turns as parents as to whose job it is tonight. Some parents are very deep sleepers and may not be aware that the child has climbed into their bed during the night. It will be especially important to stop the child from waking up in the parents' bed for reasons previously discussed. If parents are uncomfortable locking their door, then leave it ajar, but place a cow bell or wind chimes on the door that will be heard if the child opens the door more fully. Some kids are sneaky and will hold the bell as they walk in. You may need to attach the bell to the top of the door.

Giving in to the child or negotiating that they can sleep on the floor in your bedroom will only result in losing any progress previously achieved. The child learns to persist, knowing that the parents will give in eventually. When attempting to break a bad habit, be prepared for an extraordinarily strong resistance. This is called **resistance to extinction**. A child will resist giving in, working harder to control the parents and push them back into giving in. They will really try your patience. Over time, they resist less — but every so often they try again to see if you can be manipulated. Parents must stay the course and not give in, else they will quickly lose all progress. If they give in, the child's resistance will become even stronger.

While working on independent sleeping, avoid letting the child attend sleepovers either with friends or relatives. This will undo all your progress. Grandparents like to spoil grandkids. If you must depend on childcare from extended family, housekeepers, or babysitters, then make sure to include them in the treatment planning.

Social-Skills Group Therapy for Children

One of my favorite forms of psychotherapy for children involved social-skill groups. Having a social-skill group for a child gave me a controlled situation to observe the child's social level of development. Group also gave me a way to practice the new skills I had been teaching during family and individual sessions. For social skills to generalize, a child needs to practice the new skills. Role-playing during individual or family/parent homework had some limitations with the process of transferring, or generalizing, the new skill to real-life social events. Within group, there were real kids with actual social interactions to work with.

See Social Skills Group (Page 174), with the figures for Socialized Child (Page 176), and Planning a Social Event Worksheet (Page 175) in Appendix.

Many of the children I treated had extremely poor social skills due to developmental delays, such as ADHD and autism, or anxious or aggressive in-born personalities. They were awkward, overly sensitive, and had few friends. Many were targets for taunting by peers, or overreacted aggressively to frustration. The feeling of enjoying the company of same-age peers was not being experienced. Often, they became isolated, shunned by the general peer groups found at school and in the neighborhood, excluded from hobbies. Left unchecked, they could have grown up to be angry, anxious, and depressed social outcasts, never knowing the pleasure of positive interactions.

I often ran as many as eight groups a week. Groups ran from ages five through eighteen. I arranged groups by ages, separating them according to similar stages of development: ages five through six, seven through nine, ten through eleven, twelve through fourteen, and high school. With the high schoolers, I would mix genders. The younger children's groups were not mixed gender in order to help them make same-gender friends which is particularly important during the younger years. Mixing the younger groups between genders adds more pressure to the sessions. Girls like to do girl stuff, while boys like boy stuff. With high school students, the need to relate across genders is especially important.

A typical group had between six and eight kids. This size group was manageable, while having enough kids available in case a child was out due to illness. Groups met once a week for an hour session. Children usually stayed in group for a minimum of a year, while some children spent many years in group. It seemed that the members formed a support system, helping each other through the developmental years. Many of the group members also experienced their first real friendships. As a group matured, they often met for weekends to enjoy social events together, like birthdays or going to the movies. They discovered that there were many children like themselves to form their own unique social crowd at school. They accepted their own natures and sought out similar kids wherever they went, no longer feeling inferior to other established crowds, such as the so-called "popular kids."

It was important to consider the mix of child personalities within a group. For instance, a child with oppositional issues worked better with a group that did not have another oppositional child. Two or more oppositional kids often formed a sub-group that supported the disruption of a group. Preferences also had to be considered. Children are naturally attracted to different types of play, which can present a challenge with mixing and balancing fun, social activities.

Within group, I used a **token economy**. Children earned tokens to be saved up toward five-dollar gift cards from favorite stores. A token economy gave me a quick way to notice positive behavior. I tried not to take away tokens to punish bad behavior. Good behavior was the only way to gain tokens. A minimal number of tokens, however, were needed to gain credit for a positive session counting towards the gift card.

The younger groups — elementary grades — were very structured, while the middle and high school groups were more open ended. Teenage Thinkers hate structure.

The elementary age groups followed a similar approach at each session. We would sit on the carpet in a circle — no one sat in a chair. Claiming a more comfortable chair became a disruptive activity to the group. There was a chair in a corner of the office that was designated the Calm Out chair when a child emotionally needed to withdraw to a Safety Zone. If the child took that chair, they still received tokens for properly doing a Calm Out and not disturbing others.

Each session began with a positive drill, followed by various skills like handling teasing, telling a joke, giving a compliment, asserting "Why did you do that?", sharing something they had recently enjoyed, conversation drills, eye contact drills, silly acting, etc. If a child had a specific need, I stressed a drill to reflect the problem.

One of my favorite activities for the younger children involved using hula hoops. Some children could not respect the personal space of others. They would interfere, disrupt, and annoy other kids by not maintaining their position or space when playing a game. I would set up six hula hoops and each child had to stand inside their assigned ring while a balloon, ball, or stuffed animal was passed around the room. The rule was not to step out of their hoop.

At other times, two children would face each other. One would be inside the hoop and the other outside. The outside child would then enter the hoop, and the child who was already in the hoop would say assertively, "Can I have some space, please?" As the other child stepped back, they would say, "Thank you." At other times, I would have six kids in one hoop, each facing a different direction, and ask them to pick up six items scattered around the room. They had to walk as one group. Each child had to take turns giving directions to each other to move as one around the room. This activity fostered teamwork and becoming more comfortable with people within a close space.

Two more of my favorite and standard drills were the "Hot Seat" and "Sneak Attack" drills. The "Hot Seat" involved having a child sit in the center of the circle. Members of the group were encouraged to take turns teasing that child. I would sit next to the child and help them use comebacks to deflect the teases. Tokens were given for each comeback they used. Later during the group, I would use a "Sneak Attack" on a child. If they responded with a good comeback, they earned extra tokens or points. I would also take a turn in the Hot Seat and offered to be a target for Sneak Attacks. Children were told that if I got upset by the tease, they would earn $100. The kids tried hard to catch me, but, in all those years, I never paid out due to my modeling good comebacks.

Parents were asked to let me know in advance about any problems their child had that week. The parents were not directly included in the treatment room. They remained in the waiting room. Parents did help, however, when a child needed to use the bathroom or needed a Calm Out from the group room.

Following drills, I often ran a group activity that required a cooperative effort with some win-or-lose frustration involved. Children often did group juggling, silly improvisations, conversation drills, or played a sport like bowling or balloon volleyball. Additionally, the children liked to put on a play. We would work together to form a plot, create characters, and choose roles.

Within each session, one child was usually given a chance to be the leader and pick a game for the group. It could be a board game, office sport, or art or craft. The leader had to pick something we could all play, pick fair sides, make decisions, and learn to praise the group members. During a game, everyone was encouraged to cheer for each other. When the activity ended, we would sit around and give the leader praise for what they did. No criticism was given. These kids were good at criticizing others since they often heard a lot of criticism directed toward them outside of group. The leader then had to go around the group and give praise to the others. Sometimes I decided that there would not be a leader for the session. Instead, the group together had to negotiate and decide what to play. This kind of decision making was more commonly seen on the playground.

When the group at times became out of control, I would quietly sit down on the carpet and take a Calm Out. Eventually, after wasting their own time, they would resume activities with less time to play. Drills had to be done before they could do their play activity.

Another special event that was run seasonally was the "Silly Olympics." Special events were needed to break up boredom from routines. The "Silly Olympics" involved small sub-groups forming a team representing a country which they randomly pulled from a hat. They had to make up a cheer, song, and silly mascot. Silly games were created to practice teamwork and winning/losing. Points were awarded and gift cards were earned for gold, silver, or bronze.

The children learned how to creatively use imagination for fun. They were introduced to street games I had played as a child, games like knock-hockey, balloon volleyball, Hit-the-Penny, stickball using Nerf balls, indoor tennis, "Keep the Balloon off the Ground," Pods, card games, Charades, and many more. At times, I would give them a few objects and ask them to invent a game; other times we would make up new rules for a game, learning to be creative and flexible. Do-overs were encouraged as well as rock-paper-scissors to make decisions and settle differences.

Middle school and high school groups were less structured. They could sit on chairs, making for interesting observations about power positions as well as who would hide from attention. Each session usually involved going around the room and sharing some feelings or events. Skill tasks were still used, stressing How We Make a Feeling, anger management, handling teasing, and making conversations. At times, the session involved learning how to stand up to aggression. Sometimes an individual chose the game for that session, and other times the group decided what to do for fun. There were more discussions about feelings that were typical of teenage life. How to talk to the opposite gender, as well as sexuality, were important topics.

Issues of Loss: Divorce and Death

Issues of loss usually involved divorce or death of a loved one such as a parent, grandparent, sibling, or family pet. Children also experienced loss with the death of a classmate or as a result of a tragic event in the immediate neighborhood. To address these issues, both parents and children needed intervention.

A child's ability to cope within the family/country model highly depends upon the stability of the parents/government. With divorce, I have seen terrible parental behavior, such as using the children against the other parent. Divorce is hard enough, but when used as a weapon, it becomes intolerable for the child.

It is so important that each parent undertake counseling when a breakup occurs. They need to work through anger, depression, and anxiety. Whenever possible, family or couple therapy to bring about resolution is essential. The therapist involved with a parent needs to be careful not to become aligned with a parent's position in opposition to the other parent. Too often, I saw professionals taking sides and becoming an extension of parental acting-out. Therapists need to understand that there are always two sides to a story. Unfortunately, there were times I was compelled to involve authorities when a parental action was harmful to the emotional and physical needs of the child.

If parents can accept that the relationship has ended, then they can adjust to co-parenting. Each parent will handle their new, separate home in different ways. I encouraged parents to each follow the **Choose to Earn Privileges** model. It was also stressed that, when there were parenting disagreements, they should seek arbitration. I provided parents the opportunity to come in and discuss adjustments and differences together, offering my opinion on a compromise solution. This frequently helped to keep acting-out under control. I encouraged parents, when possible, to come together for a session to discuss the children. Either parent could also call me for advice regarding the treatment plan. They were instructed to communicate directly with each other and not use the children as messengers between them.

Eventually, parents began to date new partners. Dating presented additional concerns. Too often, a parent rushed the child into meeting the new person. Many times, the new person also had children. They hurriedly tried to replace the lost family with a new family. Sometimes, after a short period, the dating did not workout. The new couple split up, and the child experienced another loss. I saw some parents do this over and over to their children. My advice to parents is to date a person for at least six months to a year before involving the children. Take time to be sure that there is a good chance that your new relationship will stabilize. It is ok to tell your child you are dating and to introduce that person, but respect limits.

Grandparents and other relatives often complicate the situation by taking sides against the other parent. The child has relationships with the extended family and can feel even more loss when the extended family also breaks off from the child. You may not like your spouse, but the children may love the extended family. Help them to stay connected with each other. I also led sessions for the extended family members to help them cope with the loss. When the extended family gets polarized, it gets ugly for the child.

It is important not to alienate either parent. At times, some parents were so angry that they used therapy in order to hurt the other parent. They would refuse to continue the child's therapy when they did not get their way. I tried to establish a policy that I would only see a child going through divorce if both parents agreed to my intervention. There were still times when a parent would not agree with the child's therapy. I would see these children if the contact parent had custodial rights.

A major loss will upset a child's sense of security and safety. In the Family as a Country model, a child is dependent upon the parent/government to be in control. When the government collapses, it is felt throughout the country. Depression, anxiety, trouble sleeping, angry acting-out, and withdrawing socially are common problems exhibited by children. With young children, I used stories to highlight the changes that were occurring, and play therapy to foster security and hope. Children need to have some time to experience happy feelings and to know that there are others around to protect them. Staying lost in the hurt leads to more severe reactions.

It was also important to empower the children to set limits on their parents. Many times, children were used as messengers between the parents. Other times, they heard a parent saying angry, mean things about the other parent. I taught the children to say, "That's adult talk, not child talk." Parents were taught to expect that comment, and respect it. If a child needed some quiet time, they could request to go to their Safety Zone, especially when a parent was being too emotional.

Loss due to death as well as post-traumatic events can be extremely upsetting to a child. They can withdraw deeply, trying hard not to talk about the loss. It is important that those going through loss learn to talk about the loss. They need to know it is ok to talk anytime. Those with PTSD often try to block or suppress talking about the pain. As a therapist, my role was to establish an emotional, trusting bond.

Dreams can be another avenue into learning to express the loss. Children can be taught how to keep a dream journal. As they awaken, they can record any memories of their dreams. That can become material for discussion. Drawing pictures of a dream can also be encouraged. Another suggestion is to take memories from the dreams and write a continuing story, and, as if in a play, perhaps act out the story. For example, "The big bad bear was chasing you when..." Have the child fill out the rest of the story and put on the play.

Children dealing with loss due to death should be encouraged to place memories around them, such as pictures, mementos, and posters of shared events. It is important to remember the love they enjoyed with the missing loved one. The missing person should still be spoken about at events, such as birthdays and holidays. They have passed, but their spirit lives on!

If a child has a history of angry experiences with the deceased, it is important to teach them it is ok they were angry and might not have loved the missing person. A child may develop guilt for thinking badly of the deceased. They can learn to forgive the person, but also learn to accept it is ok if they do not feel love toward the deceased.

Perspectives on ADHD

Attention-deficit/hyperactivity disorder (ADHD) presents an exceedingly difficult challenge with respect to parenting and development. It is particularly important to stress that ADHD is a biological condition. As I explained in the section on OCD, it is as biological as I need glasses to see. You can take away my glasses and either punish or reward me to see better, but, alas, all I will get is punishment. A child with ADHD does not choose to be impulsive, unfocused, or hyperactive unless they are, perhaps, deliberately doing so, as may be the case in children with oppositional defiant disorder (ODD). The causes of ADHD are multifaceted. ADHD is a term used to summarize the collective symptoms but not the singular explanation for its causation.

I enjoyed giving talks at parenting groups on ADHD. I wanted to get the attention of parents and to highlight what a child with ADHD was going through. As a presentation was beginning, just after I was introduced, I would race around the room creating disarray and disorder. I would run up through the rows of seats, crawl under chairs — popping up randomly, climb on furniture, laugh out loud, open and close windows, take things from the audience, act as if I didn't hear anyone and, as soon as it looked like I was done, I'd do it all over again. This would go on for ten minutes. The parents all had confused looks as I returned to the podium. I, then, would proudly state, "Now you know what it feels like to be a child with ADHD, as well as a parent raising such a child." We all laughed and relaxed after my exaggerated performance. The point was made. It is exceedingly difficult for all parties.

ADHD comes with two major types: with or without hyperactivity. Impulsivity and problems with focusing attention are common components. As stated earlier, this is a biological problem of the brain's inability to keep behavior under control and regulated. The attention, focusing, and executive/planning/thinking sections of the brain are not working well. ADHD is evident before age eighteen. Adults continue to have ADHD — it is not a problem that is aged-out of. I have also met adults who had brain injuries due to an accident, resulting in ADHD-type behavior. They had to be taught to live life as if they had ADHD.

Staying on task, multi-tasking, following instructions, respecting limited time spans, declining school performance, as well as social-skill issues are common problems. Hyperactivity presents additional difficulties.

ADHD can be due to neurotransmitter deficiencies in the brain. All information throughout our bodies is sent to the brain through bio-chemical messages. These messages go up to the brain, are analyzed, and then response messages are sent out. All this happens in microseconds. Chemicals called neurotransmitters cross between two nerve cells that carry these messages. This system can become disrupted where the flow of information to the brain is inconsistent and the reaction message is not appropriate to the situation.

There are children born with deficiencies in brain functioning due to hereditary factors and/or pre-birth brain injury. ADHD often runs in families. Doing the Family as a Country assessment often revealed who the child resembled with respect to ADHD. Brain injury is not inherited but happens with the development of the brain during pregnancy. Brain injury can also be caused by birth trauma, or head injuries which can occur throughout life.

With some children, the disruption in message transmission is not solely at the brain level but begins at the sensory-input level. Some children's sensory systems consistently fail to pick up information or become quickly overloaded. Auditory and visual messages get mixed up. The child gets confused and behaves out of context. Learning disabilities are noted for some children who may have weaknesses with certain types of learning-skill tasks and, as a result, cannot focus well. They experience greater amounts of frustration in school, and their grades suffer.

Traditional classrooms may not work well for these children. They are often bright and creative kids, capable of learning, but need to be taught from a perspective that reflects their own unique sensory system or learning style. For example, I have seen children learn well when movement is included in their classrooms. I have seen children excel when a teacher presents material centered upon the child's best way of learning. In my opinion, it's better to drop the ADHD label, which emphasizes a "disorder," and focus more on individual learning styles. We are differently abled rather than disabled!

Children with ADHD often suffer from poor self-esteem. They become fearful of making mistakes and avoid challenging tasks. Many develop into underachieving adults. Anger, depression, and poor social development are also evident.

As mentioned in previous sections, ADHD behavior can also be the result of dietary problems. Some children have an adverse reaction to certain foods or additives, such as food coloring. As a result, these children sometimes become aggressive, hyperactive, or inattentive.

Frequently, ADHD is treated with medication. I accept that some children will benefit from this approach. I do believe, however, that medication has been overused. Focusing solely on medication treatment often overlooks the big picture, as revealed by the Family as a Country perspective. ADHD is a complex issue that cannot be simplified into just medication alone. There is no one pill to solve the entire problem. Medication is helpful for extreme ADHD, but management of the life of a child with ADHD is very, if not more, important as well. I have also seen many children on medication cocktails. These are combinations of prescribed medications that can have a dramatic negative impact on a developing child's affect and behavior. Problems with mood, sleep, appetite, and emotional volatility are often observed. Organizing home, school, and social relationships is still required even when a child is on medication.

The goal for raising children with ADHD is to teach them how to manage and organize their lives. They will learn organization skills from those around them, such as parents, teachers, and coaches. Everyone is unique in how they learn. Accepting our differences and growing from them makes for more capable adults. As frustrating and demanding as it can be to raise a child with ADHD, always remember these children need love and support.

Please refer to sub-sections throughout "The Age of Discovery Child" section on managing and organizing a child's environment as they are particularly relevant to children with ADHD. Structure offered in those sections is essential for children with ADHD. In the Appendix, please refer to my handout on Managing ADHD for Children (Page 178).

I have also included in the Appendix, the case study of Chris, a child with ADHD (Page 145), as viewed from the **Family as a Country** model.

Volume Two
Adults

Introduction

I would say that at least 50% of my practice involved treating adults. I enjoyed having interactions with adults as much as I enjoyed treating children. I would treat adult issues that were identified during my Family as a Country assessment. There were also many adults who came to see me whose issues were not related to children. I saw young adults struggling to get started with their lives as well as seniors dealing with end-of-life stages. Most often these individuals had problems with moods (either being anxious or depressed), problems with relationships, job-related issues, post-traumatic stress disorder, phobias, OCD, sleep disorders, or the problems of aging.

Working with children focused on developing still-emerging skills and beliefs. My work with adults involved two processes: first was undoing damaging behaviors and beliefs that had been well-ingrained over considerable years; second was developing new coping skills.

The resistance to change can be even greater for adults than children. Although many of the adults I saw came asking for help, they often wanted the easiest way to change. When faced with the understanding that considerable effort would be required, many chose not to go forward or left before making considerable progress. Unfortunately, there are no magic words or immediate, life-changing advice that will suddenly make everything right.

Resistance also came from significant people in my clients' lives, such as life partners, fellow employees, and friends. When someone starts to make changes, they are asking others to be accepting of their new behaviors. This, at times, does not go well. Others must adjust their own behaviors to accommodate the client's new behaviors. People do not like to change, so they resist and sometimes even sabotage others' efforts to change.

I would begin my assessment with a thorough discussion of background history. Two to three sessions were usually required to record history. The next stage of the process would be a clear description of the problem. It was important to understand what the behavior was, when it occurred, where it took place, and who was involved. It was also important to look at the secondary gain for the behavior or what purpose it served.

Once a thorough understanding was established, the treatment goals were set up. The patients were asked to describe what life would be like if things were better. This was often exceedingly difficult. They were so good at seeing how bad life was, they could not picture what a positive perspective would look like. With persistence, we would examine what life would look like if it were better regarding work, relationships, hobbies, health and exercise, coping skills, and long-term aging.

As I mentioned in the introduction, I employed a teaching method of therapy. Complaining endlessly was discouraged. Support and empathy were given, but learning new cognitive and behavioral skills was the focus. I would often begin with teaching about How We Make a Feeling. The focus of this program is to learn to take responsibility for behavior and feelings rather than blame others endlessly. I would introduce concepts through a series of questions. These questions were meant to challenge their way of understanding and thinking.

How Do You Make a Feeling?

In my Introduction section as well as throughout the preceding volume of my treatment perspective with children, I put forth concepts that were foundational to the treatment of adult concerns. I would like to draw the reader's attention back to sections explaining the contrast between the Experience vs. Failure roads of life (see Page 61). It would be helpful to review that material now as a precursor to the volume of adult treatment.

Whether someone was feeling anger, sadness, depression, anxiety, or even happiness, I always began adult therapy by asking this question: **How do you make a feeling**? Most often, there was a short, confusing interval followed by the return question, "What did you say?" Again, I asked, "How do you make a feeling?" Taking some pleasure in causing some confusion, I explained that their confused reaction is quite common. Most people struggled and could not seem to understand my request. Typical responses were usually, "My feelings just happen," "My feelings are a reaction," or "People do or say something that makes me feel this way." The major focus was always on an external "someone" or some event that made their feelings. I then explained that their responses were not correct and their perspective was wrong. This initial confusion began the process of breaking down the rigidity of their thinking. A challenge was made!

Most people have no understanding of how a person makes their own feelings. If we cannot understand how we make our feelings, then we cannot take any responsibility for our feelings or actions. It's easy to say, "You hurt my feelings," or "You made me angry," or "You made me feel guilty." Blame, blame, and blame! It is our rationalized response to justify our inappropriate reactions. "It is your fault that I feel so bad." We hear this everywhere around us. From conversations on TV, radio and internet, at home, school, and on the job, it is the same message: "*You* made me feel upset. It is not my fault!"

When one believes that they are externally controlled, it means that they are not responsible. This way of looking at life creates a sense of hopelessness and an inability to control and improve your own life.

I am not suggesting that others do not do things we do not like. People can act poorly towards us. It is especially important, however, to remember that we have a **choice** when it comes to our responses. I will attempt to make this clearer as we continue.

Now that I had my client's attention, my next question was: **Where in your body do you make your feelings**? Once again, there was usually a period of confusion and struggle. Common responses were, "From my heart," or stomach, head, etc. Asking for an explanation to further clarify their answer, I continued to hear confusion. It was apparent that understanding this process was a mystery. The most common wrong answer I got was that feelings come from the heart. In this country, we are obsessed with claiming the heart as the seat of our feelings.

What is the heart? The heart is a muscular organ that pumps blood throughout our bodies. It is an organ that takes its direction from the brain. The **brain** tells the heart what to do. It is the brain that is the seat of our feelings! Unfortunately, we are often unaware of the brain doing its job, but we can easily feel our heartrate change. The reaction in the heart is the last physical reaction in the feeling process. The first physical point in the process of making a feeling begins with the brain's reaction to sensory input. The heart's feeling may be used as a signal to direct our focus to the brain, but most often we do not teach people that step.

In many ways, society glorifies and perpetuates the misconception that feelings begin with the heart. We have Valentine's Day and cards with beautiful hearts. We say, "I love you with all my heart." It should be cards with pictures of brains and messages that say, "I love you with all my brain." We do not love someone if we do not like their qualities or nature. We say, "What a good, kindhearted person!" It should be, "What a good-brained person!" We say, "What a black hearted person!" Although I have objections to assigning negative connotations to "black," it is more correct to say, "What a black-brained person!"

Even when someone correctly said that feelings begin in the brain, I found most people had a profound lack of understanding of how the brain works. I challenged the strength of their conviction. The usual response I got was still confusion and uncertainty. They still believed that their feelings were caused by outside forces and, therefore, not their fault.

The Thinking Brain

Feelings and actions begin in the brain. My next question to clients was: **"What can our brains do better than lower forms of animals?"** What can we do better than dogs, lions, tigers and bears (oh my)? Usually, I would get answers like, "We can talk and communicate our needs." Yes, but we know when our dogs want to go out or want to play, as well as many other desires. The client then would say, "But we can think." Although they were closer to the correct answer, I pointed out that my pets seem to be thinking of how to get my attention for what they want from me. Finally, they admitted they did not understand. This confusion was still an important first step in the right direction.

What we do better than lower forms of animals is that we **think abstractly**. We can think in ways that can make us act **brilliantly.** We can send spaceships to the surfaces of other planets and send satellites to the moons of Jupiter and Saturn. We can take photos analyzing their surfaces and send them millions of miles back to earth in a matter of minutes. We can talk to people thousands of miles away, as if they are next door, on a cell phone that can relay our message to a satellite twenty miles up, all powered by a small battery. We can talk to someone on the other side of the planet via the internet within seconds. We can map the entire human genome. We know where all the human genes are, and we can design new medical treatments at the most basic levels. The list of how brilliantly we can think is endless.

We also can, and frequently do, think very **stupidly.** We can hate people because of the color of their skin, their religion, race, where they live, how much money they make, how they look, etc. We go to war and kill each other. We pay farmers in the USA not to grow food so the price of food will stay high so greater profits can be made by corporations, while more than half the people in the world, including people in the USA, are starving. The USA is lucky to be located on the garden spot of the planet, but we claim that it is *our* food and not *earth's* food. If you cannot pay for it, well, that is too bad. Other countries lay claim to resources as theirs and not the earth's resources. We have drugs that can control HIV, as well as many other diseases, but the drug companies charge thousands of dollars per year for treatment. In other words, if you live in a poor country or do not have health insurance coverage, then that is too bad. There is no profit in giving it out for free. Some people are raised to believe that it is justifiable to perform terrorist acts. Someone's terrorist is someone else's hero, all according to how we think.

Feelings come from how we think. It is our **philosophy of life**, our beliefs, values, and attitudes that direct our behavior and feelings. Thinking brilliantly means to see and interpret events from facts. Thinking stupidly means to take opinions and act upon them as if they are facts. For example, if you grew up in a home where everyone was prejudiced, there is a good chance you acquired the same attitudes. People having emotional difficulties are usually not thinking brilliantly.

Even if some problems are due to deficiencies in brain chemistry, it is still what one thinks that leads to actions and feelings. Since it is easier to sense the heartbeat and not so easy to notice the brain thinking, society perpetuates the wrong belief that the heart makes feelings. It is how one thinks that causes feelings and actions, not what others say or do.

We make our feelings, and we choose our actions!

How Does the Brain Work?

My therapeutic approach was to teach people about how the brain works. If people can understand that there is a process they can control, then they might be able to see that change is possible. If they are of the belief that others make their feelings and actions, then they may feel unable to change.

Next, I asked, **"Is your brain always thinking?"** Many of the responses I received suggested that many people were not sure. The answer is yes, we are always thinking. Are we even thinking when we sleep? The answer is still yes. When we sleep, our brain is doing housekeeping. It sorts through all the information we received throughout the day. Some bits of information are handled under the direction to "store it, but do not bother me about it," for example, what we had for breakfast or how many times we went to the bathroom.

Sometimes there are bits of information that the brain is not sure where to store. The brain sends us a dream. It wants us to make sense of this information so it will know where to store it whenever it is sensed again. There are times when we are sleeping and our brains really need our immediate attention. For example, often while I am sleeping, my brain is trying to get my attention that

I need to go to the bathroom. If I do not wake up easily, it will send me a dream with my character going to the bathroom. Thankfully (so far!), I have not missed those messages.

How fast does your brain think? It thinks faster than you know. It is not necessary to have an exact number, but it is important to know that, at times, we think so fast that we cannot "hear" our thoughts. We can feel the heartbeat but cannot easily be aware of our thinking — and we are always thinking!

As an example, imagine you are driving in your car and see a red light. An experienced driver will stop smoothly at the light, with extraordinarily little awareness of their thinking. The brain received the message of a red light and activated a **program** called "How to Stop a Car at a Red Light." The program calculated the correct distance and determined the amount of pressure to apply to the brakes to make a proper stop. When implemented, we execute an extraordinarily complex task with minimal necessary awareness. If you remember, when you first started to drive and you saw a red light, you became aware of many things: check mirrors, look over your shoulder, tap your brakes. You most likely needed three months to learn to stop smoothly. Once you learned the program, your thinking sped up and your reaction time improved, as well as your performance. In this instance, the key word is **program!** If you miss the red-light message, perhaps distracted by a cell phone, you will not initiate the program and will most likely have an accident.

Imagine that tomorrow you wake up and the government has changed the rules. Red now means "Go" and green means "Stop." Can you imagine what the next three months would look like on the roads? There would be confusion, accidents, and, unfortunately, people dying. Over the next three months, people would be thinking very slowly and out loud. As you leave home in the morning, someone would say, "Have a nice day and do not forget to stop on the green, not the red." There would be jingles on the radio every few minutes: "Stop on the green, not on the red." You would place a little green dancing stop sign on your dashboard. After three months, people would learn the new program and reaction time would increase to the point where it was before the program change. You would, once again, not be so aware of your thinking. The point is that, if you practice and stay aware, you will be able to replace the old program with a new one.

Why does our brain think so quickly? Can you imagine walking across the street, stopping in the middle of the road, and noticing something coming at you? Now, suppose you need twenty minutes to figure out what it is. Is it my grandma? A sandwich? A lamp? A table? A book? Eventually, you decide it is a big truck. Suppose you need another twenty minutes to decide what to do. Should I take a nap? Blow kisses? Write a letter? You eventually decide it would be wise to run. What would have happened for the last thirty-nine minutes? You wouldn't know, right? Because you would most likely be dead! We, however, don't die, because, as little children, when we went near the curb, most of our parents rushed over, raised their voices, swatted us on the rear end and taught us the program that "big things crush little things." With this program in our memory, the brain receives the image of the truck and tells us to run, all in a split second. Then you feel your heart racing.

We think quickly in order to survive. If humans did not have this capacity to think quickly, we would not have survived this long. This is an instinct that goes back to our caveman ancestors. If they did not think quickly when they encountered wild animals, they would have been eaten, and you would not be reading this. The strongest and quickest thinkers hunted the animals, while the weaker, slower thinkers became food for the animals. This quick-thinking trait is carried in our genes.

How does the brain know what is happening outside of our skulls? In microseconds, the brain picks up information from our senses. This information is sent bio-chemically up the spinal column and then the brain decides what to do with it. There are parts of the brain and central nervous system I call "**gatekeepers**" that will filter out information from our awareness based on the rules learned early in life. Therefore, information comes in from our senses, gets to the brain, then, very quickly, we think and we make a choice based on the programs we have stored away. This is the beginning of feelings!

There are conditions that affect neural functioning and can interfere or alter the information entering the brain. This is the case with Alzheimer's, attention-deficit/hyperactivity disorder, sensory impairments such as hearing and vision loss, and stroke. Decision making is affected by these conditions.

> *Our brain is processing sensory input information so quickly that we often only become aware when we feel the body's reaction. If you have a feeling, then what were you first thinking?*

Computers and the Brain

A computer is a brain designed very much like our human brains. It can think very quickly, is created with different strengths and weaknesses, can have long and short-term memory, can be flexible to add on programs to improve functioning, and varies with how fast it can work. The computer, however, still needs an Operating System (OS). This OS is a set of instructions that tells the computer what to do with the information it receives. Without an OS, the computer is basically worthless — except for maybe as a paper weight. No programs, no thinking!

The Two Roads of Life

Suppose a neophyte computer-user goes to a store and buys a basic computer to do word processing, formally known as typing. The salesperson sells them a Windows 95 OS program for their new computer. It is a "bit" out of date but can still do basic typing. The person goes home, installs the 95 OS, gives the computer instructions, and it works without a problem. Now they are extremely excited. They love computers. They eagerly want new programs and rush to the store. They look up and down the aisle and find a super-duper program. It does everything: bookkeeping, banking, calls Grandma, even does the laundry. They go home and try to install the super-duper program and, suddenly, all the data starts to get jumbled up, numbers flying everywhere, making no sense. They rush back to the store, angrily demanding their money back, complaining the computer or program is broken. The salesperson notices that, to use the super-duper program, the person needs a more advanced OS, such as Windows 10. The super-duper program is incompatible with the Windows 95 OS they originally installed. The computer cannot understand what to do and is having a nervous breakdown or, as my teenagers called it, a "brain fart."

So, for a few more dollars, the neophyte buys and installs the new Windows OS program. Now that the computer is capable of learning additional instructions, it inputs the new information and, lo and behold, the computer works without a problem. It totally forgets about the old 95 OS. No more problems, all is well. If a computer brain has a breakdown, it is typically easy to fix it. Just give it a new program or add on a new component. The computer is created/born with hardware but needs appropriate software to tell it how to function.

Now let's talk about our **brains**. We are born with hardware, certain strengths and weaknesses. We have what I call a **Brain Operating SystemS (BOSS)**. This BOSS is a set of instructions that tells us what to do in various situations. When we are born, we have hardware — our nervous systems — but have truly little extra software or programs for using our hardware. We are born virtually blank regarding how to function. Almost everything we do as adults comes from a program that has been taught to us, from basic hygiene to advanced technical skills. Some of us are born with advanced hardware that will allow us to do certain tasks better than others. We can vary with intelligence, music, art, sports, and so many other hardware tasks. The programmers who install our BOSS programs will make the difference between someone who uses their hardware to their full capacity and someone who fails to live up to their potential.

If your program is compatible with your current situation, then there is no emotional/behavioral problem. For instance, if you felt the immediate need to urinate, what would you do? Depending on where you were, you would seek out an immediate solution. Most of us would be able to quickly solve this issue. We would not spend twenty minutes working through numerous options. If, however, one is younger than two or three years old and felt the immediate need to urinate, the solution would be to let loose — hopefully in a diaper. Our hardware has been in place since birth. By around three years old, we have the ability for better control over this hardware. Parents now begin to install the software program and teach toilet skills. As time goes on, we discover the benefits of our new program. Most adults have not had an accident for many years.

If you are facing a situation that is not working out and it is not a hardware issue, then it is most likely a software or programming problem. The program you are trying to use will not work in this situation. The result can be emotionally and behaviorally painful. If I were able to "jack" into someone's brain directly, like in the classic sci-fi movie *The Matrix,* then emotional and behavioral problems could be easily overcome by simply switching out an old program for a new one. It may happen one day!

This is the issue that therapists work on. How do we get people to change their minds? If people can learn to understand and accept that there is a process by which they have become programmed, then maybe — with hard work — they can change their BOSS and feel and act differently.

***We must strive to be masters OF the programs
and not be mastered BY the programs!***

What am I saying? We make our feelings and choose to act according to the hardware we are born with and the software programs we are taught throughout our lives. For example, if you called me a horrible, awful, terrible psychologist and stormed out of my office, would I have to automatically be upset? The answer is no. I can choose to see it and react in many ways. I could say, "Gee, you're not happy with something," and show concern. Or, I could say, "Ok, you don't like the way I did something. Good luck. I hope you find what you need elsewhere," and just be disappointed. Or, I could say, "This is horrible that you don't like me! You have to like me! I'm such a bad psychologist because you don't like me!" and be very sad. Or, I could say, "This is horrible that you don't like me! I demand that you take it back, you horrible so and so!" and feel very angry.

How I am going to feel is up to me, *not* the person who called me a name. I make my feelings and choose my behavior; you make your feelings and choose your behavior. You can hurt me physically, but not by words or gestures.

How we think can cause amazing changes in how our bodies work. In some situations, we can even endure physical pain better if our mindset is positive. This is the case with people who practice martial arts and can break objects with various body parts without damaging themselves. By thinking only, without any doubt, "I am going to break this wood or brick object," the properties of the body parts adjust and are prepared to break the object without injury. Any hesitation or doubt will expose the body to considerable damage. In a more common way, this happens many times in a busy day: we bump into something and get hurt but do not register the pain or see the bruise because our mind is distracted thinking about something else. The power of thinking has also been shown to have healing powers when dealing with disease.

This is a free-choice world. Even if you put a gun to my head and said, "Sing the national anthem!" I could still say "no." I can't make you like me, and I can't even stop you from teasing me — short of killing you. **The only person I can control is myself.**

Take charge of your programming to take charge of your life!

Demanding, Catastrophizing, and Blaming (DCB)

Continuing to teach about how we make our feelings, consider how often we upset ourselves by trying to enforce our will on the universe. We often become terribly upset when the world will not comply with our wishes. We will **demand** that the world *must* or *should* do as we say. "You must like me." "I must not fail." "It should be easier."

This lack of compliance is interpreted as a **catastrophe**: it is Horrible, Awful, and Terrible **(HAT)**. We push it to the level of equating the world's lack of cooperation to that of wars, disease, and natural disasters. Most often it is far less severe than we make it out to be. It is only, at worst, Frustrating, Annoying and Disappointing **(FAD)**. I call it FAD as a play on words since a "fad" is a short-term event that quickly moves on. Fads are like the latest movie, song, or book that is currently popular. In a short time, they are less significant. In turn, FAD emotions are emotions we can more easily "make the best of." The acronyms HAT/FAD became especially important catchphrases for my clients. They learned to cue themselves to take the HAT off.

Faced with an unwilling universe, we **blame** ourselves or others to save face or make excuses. When we blame ourselves ("I am so stupid or worthless") we can become anxious and depressed. When we blame others ("It is your fault!") we often become terribly angry.

I continued to teach this understanding of DCB by proposing two experiments to my clients.

Experiment 1

At first, I calmly asked my client to levitate across the room. They often seemed confused and I said, "Just float across the office." Some tried to walk slowly, but I insisted that they must be off the ground. I waited patiently for them to comply. As they struggled with their inability, I raised my voice and demanded, "You must and ought to and should do as I say! Please levitate! This will make you feel great! Do not tell me you cannot!" I kept this up for a few minutes. Then I broke into, "This is so HAT! It is the worst thing in the world that you will not do as I say! Now, levitate!" With increased distress in my voice, I told them they were worthless and were pissing me off!

At this point, some of my clients started to apologize for their lack of compliance. Some of them were visibly shaken by my rejection. They thought they were upsetting me. I explained that they needed to calm down and that, no matter how forcefully I demanded their compliance, they would never be able to levitate no matter how hard they tried. "It is not HAT, and you did not make me upset. I made myself upset."

Experiment 2

I asked my client to go outside, stand in the middle of the turnpike, take off all their clothing, and wave at the motorists passing by. They would refuse to comply, and I quickly amplified my negative emotions. "This is the second time I am giving you good advice. Here we go again! You're pissing me off because you won't do as I say! This is worse than children dying! Don't you want to get better? This will make everything go away, and you think I'm a bad psychologist for asking you to run naked in the streets. I'm so worthless." In short, I made a stupid demand, made a big catastrophe about it, and started blaming.

By now, the point had been made. Very often we demand something, usually impossible, for the world to comply with. We become enraged, thinking that the lack of compliance is the worst thing in the world that could happen. Then we either blame ourselves or others for feeling hurt or angry. If you take time to notice, this goes on around us all the time. We hear or say things like, "You are pissing me off!" or "You should have done as I said! You are hurting my feelings!" We blame someone because of their religion, skin color, gender, or political affiliation. We stop thinking brilliantly and fall into thinking stupidly with opinions, not facts. It is so important to understand the difference between fact and opinion.

Through these experiments, I demonstrated the principle of **choice**. In Experiment 1, they had no choice. It is impossible to levitate. Yet I chose to get myself upset. I could have accepted that it is not possible for them to comply, using facts and thinking brilliantly, but my reaction was an example of stupid thinking: just because I said, "Levitate!" does not make it possible.

In Experiment 2 they had a choice. They could have done what I requested, yet they chose not to. I chose, however, to demand compliance. I put on the HAT and started blaming.

This is a free-choice world!

CPA: Child, Parent, and Adult

At this juncture of my teaching model of therapy approach, I diverted from my cognitive and behavioral track and involved concepts from ego psychology. I give credit to John Bradshaw's (1992) "inner child."

I began by asking my clients if they have a CPA. Of course, they all thought I was referring to the financial CPA. I told them I was referring to a different CPA. I explained that we all have the capacity for three people within us. The **Child**, which is programming based on our early childhood experiences; the **Parent**, which is the programs we picked up from our relationships with our parents; and the **Adult**, which relates to how well we are being controlled by Experience Road thinking. I pointed out that "Adult" is not an age, but a state of mind. Many of us have not reached "Adult" thinking, despite our ages. I have met young children with well-developed adult minds reflective of Experience Road thinkers, while I have met many older people who are still mostly governed by Child or Parent thinking, or Failure Road thinking.

The goal is to become more aware of which ego state is controlling our thinking/personality when making decisions. Knowing what state we are acting from can greatly help in changing our programming. Awareness can become a trigger to turn us toward changing our programs.

Change the programs to change our lives!

Let us take a deeper look at the CPA to gain more understanding.

The Child: This state represents the repository of our childhood experiences. I focused on our worries, fears, anxieties, and traumas. These are issues left over from childhood. We still struggle with them and they continue to be unresolved. We can never eliminate these events from our life histories. They will continue to be part of who we are and will influence our judgment and behavior. Many times, we are unaware of their influence; other times, we can become overwhelmed by these experiences.

We need to understand and use all our experiences, whether good or bad, as information to help ourselves. We cannot make our bad experiences go away. No one can remove any of their past experiences. We should strive to become a *total person*. Such a person is aware of their past events and feelings but is not rigidly controlled by them. What we *can* change is our reactions to them.

All experiences, whether good or bad, can be information to help guide us throughout our lives.

We all have what I call **exposed nerves**. We have this sensitivity alarm that we or others can set off as a signal of danger. Others may not be aware of this exposed nerve and will inadvertently trip over it, while some may deliberately attack it. When the alarm or exposed nerve is set off, there is a corresponding, biological bodily reaction, i.e. tightness in your stomach, chest, or head. It can be an increase in heart rate, or we can become sweaty or dizzy. This happens way before awareness. Remember, information comes into our senses and travels to the brain to be interpreted, all in microseconds, by gatekeepers. In addition, do not forget that we are programmed, whether inborn or learned, to be sensitive to some information we deem to be a message or signal of danger. A baby's crying is an inborn signal of danger, while a phobic reaction is a learned or acquired danger signal.

It is particularly important to become more sensitive to or aware of the biological messages that tell us that our exposed nerve has gone off. I stressed this throughout my sessions. We need to sense that special feeling that means our guard or defenses have become activated.

I examined at length what fears, anxieties, and insecurities my clients picked up during their childhoods. Accepting that they may have been carrying self-defeating attitudes that were causing them to have coping problems is better than blaming others for their problems. We make our own feelings. We can stop punishing ourselves (and the world) for not being perfect.

There are common themes that are reflective of our exposed nerves. They are the unresolved conflicts left over from childhood still actively controlling our lives. When someone's personality is dominated by the Child, they often live on the Failure Road of life. They stay overly fixated on danger. There is a fear of the loss of security within the world around them. They do not generate their own sense of security or safety.

The two most common childhood themes I have found reflect **success or failure** and **acceptance or rejection**. "I must not fail, and I must be liked or loved by everyone." Most of us have some aspects of these themes that come into play daily. When I trip over my exposed nerves, I feel tightness in my stomach and an uncomfortable feeling in my face. Others feel the nerves in different parts of the body. My body reaction has become a signal to me that, "Oops! I am doing it again. I am reacting from my Child." I calm my Child down and then use the signal to examine where the danger is and switch to the Experience Road with Adult thinking.

The Child can have an extraordinarily strong grip on a person's way of thinking and personality, to the point it can become crippling. I recall that we once had a so-called adult over for a visit, when my son came into the room with his pet snake no bigger than a pencil. Our guest ran storming out of the house, like a young child, screaming down the street about the snake. She came back to blast us for putting her in danger. How childish was her reaction!

Knowing your exposed nerve can help you teach your inner Child to feel safe and secure. When it goes off, you can use the feeling to check your thinking and work at changing the program. "It is ok. It is not HAT, it is just FAD!"

Keep in mind that not all childhood memories are bad — many are particularly good. I have used these good experiences with stress reduction and hypnosis as a coping response to desensitize anxiety.

Know your exposed nerves and learn to put them away!

The Parent: Our parents are the most dominant programmers of our attitudes, values, and beliefs. When under their roofs, we are exposed to many ways of thinking. We pick up attitudes almost unconsciously. To highlight this concept, I often asked a client how they chose their religion. They usually responded that they did not choose, but that it was what their parents believed. The same could be said for what sports team they followed. It is, unfortunately, also how we learn biases and prejudices. We often follow the family history of beliefs without challenging the validity of those ideas. We accept opinion and not fact — not brilliant thinking!

The behaviors and habits that our parents exhibited can also be modeled and never challenged or confronted. For example, programming for parenting can be "installed" early in our lives, lying dormant until we become a parent. Suddenly our parents pop out of our heads and we often repeat blindly what they did, even if it was ineffective. Some people are fortunate to have been raised by a parent with a strong, positive Adult perspective. They pick up more constructive ways of thinking and responding.

With many of my clients, the Parent could be demanding, controlling, and often inflexible. This type of Parent is on the Failure Road of life. The Parent believes or demands that the world should, must, and ought to be the way they see it. I needed to frequently stress that this world is a "sometimes" world, not an "always" world! We need to be flexible, not rigid. Rigidity leads to feeling guilty and depressed when we are not perfect. We can become terribly angry when the world does not comply and punish ourselves or punish the world.

It was important to take time to look at how my clients felt about their parents. It is helpful to see this from a learning, not a blaming, model. It was not my approach to spend years going over early childhood life, but to look at how they were affected by their parents. What of the parents' ways of life have they carried with them that are holding them back from living a happier and more fulfilling life?

The Adult: In this state of existence, a person strives to live by the principles of the Experience Road. They more often think brilliantly, basing their interpretations, decisions, and actions on facts, not opinions. They see each moment as one that can teach something. They are open to change and possibilities yet unseen.

When events are not going well, the Adult takes control of the Child or Parent within and regains self-composure. They say to their inner Child, "Take my hand. We will get through it together." They provide themselves with a sense of security. "It's not HAT. Let's see what we can do." Just like a good parent teaching a young child not to be afraid of the dark, I taught my clients to take their own hands in hand as a gesture that calms their inner Child.

In summation, I took the time to teach my clients how the brain works, how we make our feelings, old versus new programming, and what level of ego state (CPA) was governing their lives. I used this new foundation of skills to tackle problems, either individually or as a couple.

Are you controlled by Child, Parent, or Adult?

The Attack of the Killer ANTS

As I progressed with treatment goals, I would continue to teach my clients new ways of coping and to conceptualize the central philosophy guiding their treatment. The main treatment goals usually reflected new behaviors and resolution of conflicts. I also set a goal that my clients be able to help themselves by learning a heathier way of thinking. I tried to give them an understanding that translated into self-help skills.

When addressing issues such as depression and anxiety, it is essential to gain control over how one thinks. As a person sinks into depression or anxiety, their thoughts become darker and darker, more and more negative. Another helpful way to tackle obsessing over antagonistic, negative thoughts (**ANTS**) is to use

humor to stop the thoughts from taking control of our minds. When we put ourselves down or get emotionally riled up, we are thinking many HAT thoughts. The longer we are focused on this way of thinking, the worse our emotional/behavioral condition becomes. I used the acronym ANTS as a suggestion that these thoughts are "mind insects."

Some of us had an Uncle Milton Ant Farm as a childhood hobby. You'd purchased a thin plastic chamber, about 12x10x1 inches. The chamber included sand and supplies for a successful ant colony. You then sent away for the ants which were delivered within a few weeks. They came in a small test tube, about a dozen ants. Opening the top, you placed the ants within the chamber and sat back to watch. Within hours, they began to dig tunnels and a community developed. There were worker ants and leadership ants. They held community meetings, grew food, and even buried their dead.

Now, picture a negative thought beginning to invade you brain/mind. It begins simply but starts to grow into more thoughts, branching out and tunneling into your consciousness, totally invading your focus. If left unchecked, these thoughts consume your attention, leading to unhappy emotions or actions. Just like an ant colony taking over the chamber, these thoughts burrow throughout your brain while taking over your thinking.

Imagine you are at home in your kitchen when you spy an ant walking across your countertop. Our most typical response is to smash it. We cannot let it get back to the colony and bring back more friends. Then, picture yourself becoming aware of an **antagonistic, negative thought (ANT)** crossing your awareness. As if in a silly cartoon, picture a giant rubber hammer popping out of your head to smash this thought. "I can't let it get loose to grow into a negative thought colony." Laugh and enjoy the triumph of vanquishing that ANT.

Using techniques from hypnosis to visualization, I practiced repeatedly many scenarios with my clients in which they would see themselves becoming aware of an ANT and humorously smashing it. Once it was smashed, they could shift their attention into more brilliant thinking, consistent with the Experience Road.

Over the many years of my practice, I advocated using humor for a variety of mental health issues. Humor helps make it easier to confront the absurdity of some of our self-destructive thoughts and behaviors. Try to get a good dose of humor each day to relieve stress. Remember a silly story, movie, or comic strip. When you feel overwhelmed, get up and dance around and sing a silly song.

Humor helps to keep perspective!

Finding Your WOW and the Meaning of Life

So often I had to invent new ways to help my clients make sense of their daily life experiences. So much of their mindset was tuned in to being a negative thinker. Their life had become a burdensome drag of endless unhappiness. Although at times we can all lose our positive perspectives, these individuals would sink lower and lower until there was no sunshine in their daily vison. While others could find a way to get back to the sunshine of their lives, my clients more often could not find that ray of positivity.

To find that sunny path, I created the concept of **WOW**. I began by asking clients what brought them a feeling of "Wow!" As usual, when I posed this question, there was often confusion. Clarifying, I said, "Do you remember a moment when you did something and said out loud to yourself, 'Wow'?" I asked them to recall and focus on that incredibly positive, emotional experience. The hectic pace at which most of us live our lives can create tremendous stress. Our remarkably busy lives can reduce our experience of WOW and the ability to find WOW in our daily lives. WOW is the excitement found in daily experiences. WOW is when you can feel and say that something is so cool. WOW is finding the meaning and thrill of life, either in its tiny moments or grandest scale.

Without enough WOW, we experience more UGH. Daily life becomes more and more ugly, consumed with needless complaints and meaningless aggravations. Focusing on UGH leads to a suffocating, stressful, unhealthy existence.

The **WOW Factor** is the ratio of WOW, or positive experiences, to UGH, or negative experiences. Every day it is possible to find WOW. It is right in front of you. Even if you look up to the sky and see a dark cloud, try not to see it as foreboding but as nature's amazing, earthly creation. The sky is an artist's palate of shades.

The journey of life is to find your WOW. Be aware that WOW can be felt through an expansion of our sensory world. This perspective is very much the basis of the popular "mindfulness" concept (Hanh, 1975). I tried to teach my clients to expand their sensory intake of life experiences. To help them gain this perspective, I took them on a ten-minute walk around my garden, stopping in front of a few flowering plants. I asked them to try to see the colors, smell the scents, feel the textures, and watch the insects going about their lives. "Notice your breathing; listen to the sounds of birds; feel the breeze, and see the light around you."

Take a moment to taste your food rather than gulp it down. Feel a good stretch. Enjoy an inviting shower. Look at your smile in the mirror. Hug your loved ones. WOW is in these daily, small experiences.

Life can become overwhelming at times. In these moments, we need to step back from our routine situations to decompress and get in touch with WOW. After a busy week of focusing on everyone else's life problems, I found that I needed to take Saturday off and go on a hike. I led hikes for a local hiking club and, as we followed a trail, I often asked everyone to stop, focus on their breathing, look around, listen, and smell. Within minutes, we became aware of a totally different world going on around us: sounds of birds, frogs, and insects, rock formations, wildflowers, the colors of the sky, and our bodily sensations. This is the essence of what is today called "forest bathing." After a good day in the woods soaking up this contrasting existence, our minds became clearer, and solutions to problems came easier.

WOW can be found by developing passions. I often asked my clients what they felt passionate about. "What turns you on or lights up your day?" Emotionally healthier people have many passions and find pleasure in activities like gardening, cooking, painting, crafting, exercise, etc.

From a neurological perspective, when we engage in a passion, we stop obsessing on negative thoughts that initiate our emergency, bio-chemical, fight-or-flight response. When this reflex gets triggered, the body releases adrenaline into our blood stream, preparing for danger. As it builds up, our bodies tighten and our breathing becomes shallow, allowing less oxygen to get to our brains. Consequently, thinking becomes harder and our focus becomes limited to what is pulling the (usually) false alarm. Spending a WOW day in the woods can reduce tension, shut down the alarm, increase brain power, and improve our problem solving.

When our UGH vastly outweighs our WOW, we might need to step away even more. I found that taking my camera out for the day, without others along, allowed me to stop over-focusing on issues and clear my mind. Taking time to see the world through the small viewfinder of my camera helped me notice more of the little things of life's WOW that I was missing. I also found that I could be my own best friend. I did not need to have someone around to validate my existence.

Sometimes, if our UGH levels are intense, then we must step back even farther. Try going on a vacation to some place you have never been, taking up a new hobby, or developing a new skill.

The biggest roadblock to recapturing our WOW is unresolved, major conflict. WOW is often blocked by living with silent anger. When we are terribly upset, we often bury the issues rather than bring about conflict resolution. We can get stuck on the Failure Road, afraid of the "what-ifs." Even if the events we confront will lead to major life changes, such as ending a relationship or changing jobs, the Experience Road will give us hope.

WOW can be found from the smallest events and experiences to great, new, bold experiences. When our WOW/UGH ratio is out of balance, we can find our way back to more WOW if we try to catch the ANTS or HAT thoughts, notice which road we are on, and observe what is going on around us. When there are major issues, we must be brave enough to confront them. Anger will suppress all other emotions. Silent anger will harm us greatly.

Find your daily WOW!

White Blood Cells vs. Viruses

So many of my clients, particularly those with depression, had an exceedingly difficult time finding meaning in their lives. They seemed to be lost in the grand theme of existence. "Why am I here? What purpose does my existence have? Why bother to work hard to change? Life is too short."

Indeed, these feelings are quite common. People who cope better have found a purpose and justification to embrace life. Those in pain cannot seem to find a guiding principle to make sense of their short time on earth. Some people have a faith concept that guides them. I could not give my clients any religious perspective, yet I had to explain a purpose to life that could guide them. Finding an answer to this conflict encouraged me to develop a model that provided a way of understanding this thing called "life." I constructed the following model that made sense to me, and hopefully to my clients.

The first principle is that life is short. When one considers the number of years the average person lives against the vast amount of time that has passed throughout our earth's history, it is evident that we only have a short stay. Countless numbers of people have come before us and, hopefully, many more will live after us. Our time is extremely limited relative to the billions of years that have passed before our personal arrival. This is a fact we must first accept. Somewhere, in some place, our time will end. We cannot control that, but we can control how we live our lives.

Life is short!

The second principle we need to embrace is that life is a miracle. Let us consider the following: Why is it that, with our scientific ability to look out amongst the cosmos, we don't see a vastness of smiling, waving aliens inviting us to visit? Space seems very barren. Life does not seem very abundant. There may be life elsewhere, but it is hard to see it. The earth, our home, is located ninety-three million miles from our sun. It is incredible that, for life to have developed here, it took an improbable balance and mixing of many, many factors and variables. The odds of life happening here are just as great as that of it not happening. Let that settle in for a moment to process the import or meaning.

Life is indeed a miracle. It is important to take pleasure in honoring this incredible event. We, for whatever reason, have been given a gift of life to cherish and honor. See yourself as a manifestation of this miracle. We have god-like abilities to create life and grow our existence. Unfortunately, we can also destroy life. There is a choice, as guardians of this miracle, as to how we use our god-like powers.

Life is a miracle! I am a miracle!

The third principle is to understand our place in humanity's journey, from our primitive caveman days to life amongst the stars, to an age when we might be able to provide for all our essential human needs. To better understand this concept, I like to draw an analogy between the health of our physical bodies and the health of humanity as a body.

Let us first consider the health of an individual body. At any moment, within our bodies, there are a vast number of **viruses** that are attacking us and can make us ill or even kill us. We also have **white blood cells** that are working hard to keep us alive and healthy. There is a constant play of balances between viruses and white blood cells. Sometimes the viruses are winning, and we become ill, and at other times the white blood cells are winning, and we remain healthy.

Consider humanity on our planet as one total, living body. Within this body are people who act like viruses, bringing harm and destruction to humanity. They are driven by extreme negative emotions like greed and inferiority. They produce wars, catastrophic abuse of our limited resources, and divisiveness among the various races of people. There are also people on this planet whose lives are centered on healthier, more positive emotions and values. They bring about goodness, kindness, and loving acceptance of others. They try to enhance the lives they interact with daily. These people are like the white blood cells, offering that balance that keeps humanity from destruction.

Over my many years in practice, I interacted with thousands of people. I estimate that 99% benefitted from my interaction or involvement in their lives. They, in turn, would go home or to work feeling better and would pass along this good feeling to at least five people they interacted with. It could have been by showing love to their families or simply showing courtesy to a passing stranger. In a sense, I directly and indirectly enhanced the lives of thousands of other people. At the same time, there were mean, hurtful people my clients also interacted with. In turn, those negative people may have harmfully affected, both directly and indirectly, a vast amount of people.

There is one human race. We are part of a large, ever-developing species. We are on a journey together to reach our highest level of potential development. Some of us act like white blood cells, while others act like viruses. I see myself as a white blood cell. In my short time on earth, I would like to believe that my life's contribution is to be a balm to humanity, to help move us along in a heathier manner. The journey of humanity is a constant struggle between the white blood cell people and the virus people. I don't want the viruses to win.

I do not profess to understand the complexity of faith in God. Each religion has meaningful, positive guidance to help us live together. I accepted my client's wishes to worship in their own ways. I believe that, if there is a god, then living as a white blood cell could only improve my odds of getting into heaven. If there is no god, I am still better off as a white blood cell.

I choose to be a white blood cell. I take my miracle and see what I can accomplish with the gift I was given. I am connected to the larger human experience and a contributor to humanity's ultimate destination. From the days of the caveman to the future, we all have a place in this experience called humanity's journey.

The choice is yours: white blood cell or virus?

Forgiveness

Another major obstacle to a healthy relationship and inner peace is unforgiveness. We need to learn to forgive those in our past and current life, and our own shortcomings as well. Anger from holding a grudge can be so powerful that it will dominate our lives and suppress happier emotions. Anger shuts us down. Unresolved anger suppresses all other emotions.

All of us can look back at hurtful relationships we have experienced. We could have anger at our parents, siblings, and friends, or anger in a current relationship where our partner has slipped up and acted inappropriately. I want to clarify that my role is not to say that past events are acceptable. Many events are quite bad. I am primarily concerned with the ability to let go of the anger. We can live better with FAD: frustration, annoyance, and disappointment emotions, rather than HAT: horrible, awful, and terrible feelings. We can try to learn from those negative experiences. Carrying anger is a heavy burden.

To demonstrate my point, I often asked my clients to hold their arms out like they were carrying something heavy. They were told to imagine the weight. I then asked them to imagine I was offering them something very yummy to eat, while they still held up the imaginary heavy object. To enjoy the feeling of the "yummy," they had to choose to drop the weighty object or forgo the pleasure of the treat. It is the same with anger. It is too heavy a load to carry. We lose precious time to enjoy life's yummies if we stubbornly hold on to the anger.

Another way I tried to demonstrate my point was to draw a circle on a blank page. This circle represents the total amount of our emotional energy — the energy we use to relate to the world. I also drew a box in the center of the circle. The box holds painful or angry memories and experiences. These bad emotions want to break out of the box, but we are afraid to release them to rise to our awareness. We then take energy from our emotional world and build thicker and thicker walls around the box. We invest so much of our emotional energy in these walls that little is left to feel anything except the anger being used to suppress the emotions in the box. The box gets larger and larger, taking up more and more of our emotional space. The walls need to come down to free up emotional energy for more constructive, positive emotional experiences.

I want to emphasize again that overcoming early childhood abuse is hard. What happened was not fair. Carrying a lifelong, angry crusade, obsessed with the angry victim role, is a choice. What happened was awfully bad, but what we do with the feelings is our decision.

Do not wall off your painful experiences. Use them to become stronger!

I noticed that many of my clients had held hatred toward their parents for years and years. They often addressed their parents without reference to them as even having first names. It is quite common for little children to view parents as if they are devoid of personal lives. But my adult clients were still consumed with a Child-Parent conflict, holding on to hate/anger. They made comments like, "Mom and Dad should not have done this," or, "acted that way." They were supposed to have acted differently. They should have followed a "Disneyland" fantasy of behavior. There was no willingness to understand what their parents' lives were like. They could not grow into an Adult ego state until they could find a way to let go and forgive.

Two of my treatment procedures I called "They Have a First Name" and "Walk in Their Shoes." I would often share an important aspect of my life to demonstrate these approaches. I believe there is a time in therapy when sharing the therapist's experience and showing how we addressed painful issues can be helpful. Authenticity and honesty help clients to gain hope and direction. Modeling courage and Adult thinking is supportive.

This is the story of Steve and Barbara, my parents:

Everyone has a life story. This is my mine. I grew up in a household in which love was a bad, four-letter word. I spent many a night crying at bedtime. My parents were not kind to my sister and me. Mom was a specialist in throwing guilt, while Dad was very heavy-handed. Positive attention was not readily given. I also lost my dad when I was thirteen to an unbelievably bad, violent tragedy that happened to him while on his job. I spent my teen years turning away from my better friends and seeking out other angry and depressed peers. I lost myself in drinking, drugs, and rebellion. Therapy was never offered as an option at that time of my life. The result of these years was a withdrawn, socially anxious, under- achieving person. I hated my parents. My sister and I fought as well.

I held together partly due to my being a drummer in a rock band and my love for reading science fiction. My maternal grandfather was a major source of love and support, but he passed shortly after my father's passing. In my later teen years, I got some support from an uncle who came around to spend time with me until he moved away when I was seventeen. My other source of support came later, when my mom settled in with a good man. I initially gave him hell, but he eventually spent thirty-five good years in my life. Still, the early-childhood exposed nerves were in place. I still work at checking those nerves when they come out. Remember, we can never get rid of our experiences, good or bad, but we can learn to use them to make Adult decisions.

Forming relationships and being emotionally open were hard things to do. Everyone sensed an emotional wall around me. I avoided getting close to others. I did manage to hold on to a C average in high school. Everyone saw my potential except me. I went to college because I had no idea of what else to do — and to avoid being drafted into the army. It was the time of the Vietnam War. I genuinely believed the Vietnam War was immoral and joined in the loud protests of my generation.

I did very poorly in my first year of college and, as I was flunking out, I got a notice I was being drafted. My mother had wanted me to go to college to be a dentist. I was not able to grasp the science classes, as well as most classes that first year. I was luckily given a probationary status period by my college and avoided the draft. I had heard my wake-up call. I had to take control of my life before someone else did. I took classes in subjects I never heard of, like psychology. It was love at first sight! I really connected to the subject. I pledged to work hard and got straight A's for the next three years. Psychology opened me up to understanding what was going on in my head. Becoming a psychologist was, in part, *my* therapy.

I would be remiss if I did not credit my first wife, whom I met while in college, and her family for my turnaround. We had a good run until later life issues caught up with us.

As I moved on with my psychology studies into grad school, I became aware of my shortcomings and the need to bring down my emotional walls. It was time to address my anger toward my parents. At that point I knew of my parents' past lives but, like a child, never really understood what was driving their behavior. Why wasn't I good enough for my father's attention? Why was my mother incapable of warmth? To grow was to see them from a new perspective. I had to see them as **first name people,** Steve and Barbara, and understand what it was like to **walk in their shoes**.

Steve and Barbara grew up in the Holocaust. They were in their late teens when World War II destroyed their world. My father was a survivor of Buchenwald, one of the worst Nazi death camps. He lost nearly everyone except one brother. He lost his twin brother, my name sake. My mom and most of her family survived in work camps since they were cooks and bakers. She and her sister, however, had to endure abuses while in captivity.

Prior to the war, growing up in Hungary and Czechoslovakia, they had loving families. All at once everything was violently shattered. After being liberated, my parents met in a relocation camp and quickly married. My sister is four years older than I am and was born in Germany. Then they came to America, where I was born. Like most of the immigrants of the time, they possessed little and worked any way they could to survive. Life was not easy. Mom sewed dresses for wealthy women while Dad found his way working in gas stations. They worked hard and eventually moved into their own home. Life was hard in that there was little money except for food and shelter.

They slowly connected to the community we lived in and began to socialize. They were thought of as genuinely nice people in the community. At home, they were not so nice. We were taught not to trust others, not to get too close, and not to express an opinion. My parents could not foster loving feelings. They were still working through their anger and post-traumatic stress. Their anger suppressed their love. Dad refused to get close out of fear of losing loved ones again. His violent death set us all back, just at a time when he seemed to be making good strides in his own recovery.

My parents had first names: Steve and Barbara. To walk in their shoes was unimaginable. I can never personally fathom the horrors they experienced. How could I hate them? They did the best they could. I dropped the anger, however I did not find myself loving them more. Love was not an experience I had with them, but hate was no longer a feeling I needed to carry. My emotional barriers were coming down. I accepted their rejections without viewing myself as a reject. I still work on my exposed nerves, as we all must do, but I was able to see some important lessons they taught me. One such lesson was that you must keep trying and working harder to make things better, no matter how bad events are. You pick yourself up and keep going forward. Indeed, I do pride myself as a hard worker.

My awareness of my emotions has made me a better father to my children and enabled me to help other men be better fathers to the children who were my clients. Telling my story to adult patients helped them to be open about their stories and heal their exposed nerves. I have heard so many equally tragic life stories.

To forgive ourselves means to accept our imperfections, to stop trying to please everyone, and to develop a better self-image. Some of my clients were able to embrace the Experience Road philosophy and took strength from what had happened to them, while some were reluctant to give up the Failure Road and chose to stay on the victim path.

It is possible to forgive and let go of the past and its control over the present!

Couple Therapy: Marital and Partner Relationships

As I noted in Volume One, the **Family as a Country** model often revealed conflicts between parents that required marital relationship treatment. On other occasions, couples came to see me directly, without having a specific child issue. Working together with both partners was an attempt to teach them how to help each other. When teaching skills, I wanted to be sure they both heard the same message.

I was also concerned that separating the couple and seeing them individually was a threat to confidentiality and could cause some clients to try to manipulate me into joining them against their partner. I could not hold someone's secrets while having to face their partner. It's especially important to avoid becoming biased. Too often I came across therapists who had allied with one partner and became biased against the other partner/parent. These therapists seemed to be projecting their own bad experiences into the treatment.

I did see adults individually for marital or relationship issues when only one member of the couple wanted to participate. Later, when the other partner joined in, I often had to refer the couple to another therapist to avoid bias. I could not comfortably keep secrets against the other partner. I found, on occasion, through clever questioning by the other partner, I was unable to hold secrets. They were able to manipulate me into a position that my silence could be construed as an affirmative answer to their suspicions. It was essential to try to establish a sense of trust that I was not biased. When secrets such as affairs were revealed, it was then possible to see both people comfortably. Couple therapy required exceedingly difficult decisions at times.

When a client had considerable individual issues, it was necessary to refer them to another therapist while I worked only with them as a couple. It was possible to see an individual for non-related marital issues, such as phobias or anxiety, when the couple agreed the needs of the partner in question could be handled without bias.

Some couples came for advice on how to work through a divorce without hurting each other or the children. I served as a mediator, listening to both viewpoints and trying to negotiate compromises. I also taught parenting skills to bring about a common parenting model. I became an advisor they could both come to for guidance throughout and after the divorce, particularly with managing children. They were also taught the dos and don'ts about dating, visitation, and extended families. Please refer the section in Volume One regarding children and divorce, "Issues of Loss: Divorce and Death," for additional information.

Most of my clients with marital issues weren't so cooperative with each other, to say the least. They would come in wanting to do battle. One would try to convince me that they were right and the other person was the problem. The first step was to establish the rules in my office. If arguing became too intense, I often stood up and walked away from them. In such situations, I was not going to be a referee. If they wanted to stay together, we moved on to teaching skills. If they wanted to separate, then it was necessary to move on with the separation/divorce process rather than waste time beating each other up.

Couples were told that, if they really wanted to improve their relationship, they needed to commit to at least a year in therapy. Initially, weekly sessions would be required for many months. Eventually, sessions could become spaced farther apart, depending on their progress. It was important that the couple realized how much effort would be needed to grow their relationship. There was no quick fix. This was a difficult issue to face when starting therapy. More often, all the couple wanted to do was argue. When it became apparent how much work needed to be done, some clients became sensible and ended the relationship, admitting they had only wanted to separate while trying to look like the aggrieved party.

No quick fixes! You must commit!

Skills-based Model of Couple Therapy

Most individuals come into a relationship with a degree of history. It can be their first marriage or serious relationship, or they may have had multiple marriages. Some have a history of many failed dating relationships. They have learned relationship programs of what to expect or how to act based on their own parent-child experiences, society's messages, and other role models. The main issues are often a lack of ability for controlling emotions, communication, and problem solving. My teaching approach set out four skills I taught as the primary treatment goals:

> **Skill 1**: Be aware that you make your own feelings and reactions, and you alone choose your behavior
> **Skill 2**: Know that biological reactions will interfere if not addressed when they occur
> **Skill 3**: Listen and communicate needs, interests, and desires
> **Skill 4**: Problem solving

I began couple therapy by taking an extensive personal and family history from each participant. Background was collected and shared together. It was particularly important for the couple to hear each other's life story to try to establish empathy and understanding. My clients were frequently self-centered. "I am the only one with feelings. I don't want to hear your feelings. I just want the attention on me." They perpetuated a "poor me" attitude. My goal was to start moving them toward becoming other-centered. They needed to hear each other's story to realize they each had issues to confront.

Getting into a teaching model was not easy to accomplish. Most of my clients only wanted to fight and place blame. Considerable effort was needed to assure them there would be time to discuss issues when they had some better command of their new skills. They were frequently reminded to slow down and be patient. We cannot keep relating the same way repeatedly. The goal was to develop a solutions-based, problem-solving approach to life. To get to that stage, they needed to maintain self-control, calm down, and listen better. Without these three steps there could not be productive problem solving or conflict resolution.

Have patience! Learning new skills takes time!

Skill 1 reflects what I mentioned earlier regarding **How We Make a Feeling**. The concept of HAT became a particularly good catch phrase to use to regain perspective. It was extremely important that the essence of this concept be understood. The way we feel is based on how we think. We have a choice to think differently. It is essential to be able to identify Child, Parent, and Adult ego states. Each state has its own pattern or way of thinking.

Skill 2 reflects our **biological reaction** to how we think. Our sensory system and exposed nerves are triggered by what we perceive as a threat. We instantly get a surge of adrenalin entering our blood stream, making us stronger and hyper-alert. In the case of real danger, our body will go into the inborn fight-or-flight emergency survival response. If the threat is real, we will have plenty of energy to protect ourselves.

The problem is when there is no threat, but we think there is. The same alarm goes off and our bodies go into survival mode. Our muscles will get tight. Breathing is shallow and faster. As a result, less oxygen is getting to our brains, causing us to focus only on the alarm. To resume rational thinking, we must regain control over our bodies and shut off the alarm. This can take as little as a few minutes to, perhaps, a day or so, depending on how severe our thinking was affected by the alarm. Until calmness returns, the brain's ability to do problem solving is diminished or impaired. We can illustrate this situation with a sports analogy. On a sports team, there is a coach or manager whose job it is to get the best performance out of their players. Consider a basketball game. During the game, suddenly the team is doing poorly. Players begin to panic, and the game gets further out of control. The coach calls a time out and the players are led off the playing field as water and towels are distributed. The coach does not start talking until a few minutes go by. During this interval, a well-conditioned athlete may be able to get their body back under control. If a player cannot regain control, then a substitute takes over. A version of this scene frequently takes place on all sports teams. Players know that too much adrenaline can poorly affect one's performance. A clear mind and calm body work best with all sports.

The sports example teaches us that, when two people become overwhelmed by non-productive thinking as their exposed nerves are activated, they will lose control of their rational thinking. They can become hyper-emotional and biologically out of control. During our sessions, I became the coach and called for a time out. I tried to teach my clients to recognize the body sensations that reflect losing control, such as loud voices, body tension, losing eye contact, waving arms and legs, etc. They were instructed that, when they noticed these things happening, someone should make the "T" sign. That means take a time out. We must respect the "T" sign. Even if one person feels calm, their partner may be losing control. Nothing productive will occur when our nerves are firing away.

Lose control of your body and you lose control of your thinking!

Recall that **the first step in anger management is to step back to a Safety Zone**. Move away from the situation and give yourself some space to get your breathing under control. I reviewed this when I discussed anger management with children (see Volume One "Anger and Frustration Control: A Four-Step Program"). It is the same four steps: stop, step back to a Safety Zone, breathe, and think. How far and how long to step back depends on the intensity of the adrenaline rush. It may mean only a few minutes after a short walk to the bathroom, or it may mean a long walk on the beach. I must emphasize that one should not drive when in an intense, angry state. It is better to take a long walk around the neighborhood, stomping your feet for a few blocks, and then slowing down to catch your breath. Some people just need to be left alone in a place where they can feel safe for a while.

Once the adrenaline wanes and you regain rational thinking, ask yourself "What was my partner trying to say?" Try to gain some insight as to what they were trying to express. Do not reengage until you are both ready to talk calmly. If one of you is ready but the other is not, then alarms could go off again. A willingness to regain composure and return to conversation can be a positive signal to your partner that trust can be established.

When arguing persists, then partners never feel safe or trusting of each other. They may never allow themselves to be vulnerable. Some couples refuse to let their guards down out of fear they will be hurt. They often withdraw into silent anger. They drift farther and farther apart, building an angry wall between them. The silence is so thick it can be cut with a knife. Swallowing our anger is costly to our bodies and to interactions with the world.

Avoid living in silent anger!

If we can think brilliantly and can keep our bodies under control, then we are on the path to problem solving. There is still one more skill to learn before getting to conflict resolution. We need to be able to express our concerns maturely and trust that our partner is trying to understand where we are coming from.

Skill 3 is to apply **active listening** concepts and improve expressive communication skills. In Volume One, I explained how a parent can help their child clarify what their needs and issues are by using active listening (see "Active Listening and Problem Solving"). This is the same between any two adults. When someone is irrationally ranting, they have regressed to Child mode. A good partner realizes this and tries to help their partner become calm and express their issues. Shouting at your partner, as with a parent shouting at a child, will result in more intense conflict. If one has enough self-control, they need to assume the Adult state to help settle things down. If no one can reach Adult thinking, then stay in time-out until you get to your coach/therapist.

I have found that many couples in distress are locked into conflicts that started way back in childhood. They often find a partner to symbolically continue battling their parents while projecting these conflicts into the current relationship. They are dominated by Child or Parent ego states. They have not matured into an Adult ego, even if they are legally considered to be an adult.

Remember: "Adult" is a state of mind, not age!

Active listening is mirroring or reflecting what you hear, even if you do not agree with what is being said. Reflecting and staying calm can also lend your even temperament to your partner and assist them in regaining self-control. One needs to reflect the emotions before trying to get to the underlying content. I often heard my clients say that their partner does not validate their feelings, they do not acknowledge the emotions. If they feel invalidated, they likely shout even more persistently or withdraw into silent anger.

Try to hold back on taking a Parent state, demanding to know what is wrong. Stay Adult, wait for the adrenaline to subside and for rational thinking to return. Check your own exposed nerves and work on your breathing while waiting for your partner to catch up. During this time, reflect to your partner the emotions you are hearing. Use comments like, "Ok, you seem very angry at me," or "Wow, you're so very upset." Don't say, "I hear you." That can mean, "Shut up! I don't want to hear you." It is not easy to reflect unpleasant, intense emotions when you are the subject of the feelings being expressed. If you lose control, then remember to use the "T" sign and give each other some space. Hang up a reminder sign with a big "T" on the bathroom mirror or fridge as a reminder to use the Calm Out. Make a contract to respect the "T" sign.

As you both calm down, continue to encourage your partner to express their concerns. Do not interrupt each other to express your opposing agendas. When your partner has completed their comments, reflect the information you have gathered. Here are some examples: "Ok, so you are angry at me because I didn't call." "You feel I take you for granted." "You are worried that I am not interested in you." "You're afraid I don't love you." "Other past relationships have hurt you." "You feel we don't spend as much time together like we did when we first met." "You're unhappy we are not having as much sex anymore." "Our friends are getting divorced, and you are worried about us."

As you can see, the progression of reflections gets deeper into the anxiety or worry that your partner may be experiencing. While listening to your partner, it is tempting to cut them off and start in with your grievances or explanations.

Avoid slipping into your Child ego state. Stay Adult and help your partner to feel they have been heard and understood. This does not mean you are agreeing to their comments, but if someone feels heard, they are more apt to listen to your side. You can work out solutions in the problem-solving phase.

Patiently listen and reflect.

Improving expressive communication skills involves trying to say what you want in an assertive, Adult manner. There are positive and negative ways of communicating your needs that reflect your ego state — Child, Parent, or Adult.

If your personality is dominated by a hurt and angry **Child**, then you are apt to over-react. You may act like an aggressive child, crying excessively or demanding angrily. The Child can also withdraw into silence, taking the passive "I am upset, but I will not tell you" approach. Over time, it is exceedingly difficult to stay with someone who explodes or withholds. For example:

> Q. "What is the matter? You seem upset."
> A. "I don't know." "You know why." "I don't want to talk about it." "Stop annoying me." "You really pissed me off." Or, the silent treatment.

If your nature is to be a controlling **Parent,** then you are apt to become incredibly angry or demand immediate answers. There can be threats of guilt, rejection, and ultimatums. For example, "If you don't tell me right now, then I am leaving and you'll be all alone," or "You're such a baby, so annoying!" or "You are always complaining! What now?"

As I previously mentioned, some couples are locked into the destructive Child-Parent conflict. Sometimes they even switch roles, taking turns being the Child or Parent. This is the hard work of couple therapy. It can take many, many sessions of coaching to bring to awareness these destructive personality issues. Knowing why you have these exposed nerves is especially important. We need to know the triggers that set us off. Learning how to calm down and put the nerve away is an important step toward Adult.

Gain control over exposed nerves!

The **Adult** takes an assertive style. They try to express concerns in a way that is not threatening and leaves the door open for discussion. They communicate with "I" comments rather than blaming comments. The Adult accepts they are making their own feelings and can control the message. They express themselves in a way that invites a response. The message is given clearly and with appropriate emotion. Emotionally, the Adult will express FAD rather than

HAT comments. Some examples: "I am kind of disappointed with what just happened. Can we talk about it?" "It's frustrating we are not understanding each other." "It's annoying when you don't include me in important discussions."

Skill 4 is to learn how to do **problem solving**. If couples in conflict learn to stay Adult and hear each other's messages, they have a better chance of reaching a positive resolution. Good problem solving involves a willingness to compromise. Each person accepts that it is a "sometimes" world, not an "always" world. In Volume One, with respect to the needs of the parents in the Family as Country model (see "The Government: Needs of the Parents"), I used the "pizza theory" to make my point. It is worth repeating. I asked my clients to consider how we share a pizza. When you are single, you can eat the whole pie. As a couple, you get half the pie. With kids included, you get a slice. It is usually better to get some of what you want rather than risk getting none. A person can choose to want everything their way, but an Adult-based relationship will not last under that condition.

There can also be times when each person may have a vastly different take on an issue. Problem solving may also involve agreeing to get more advice from a professional, whether it is home repairs, vacation plans, or psychological issues. Seeking arbitration is a good decision.

Once issues are identified, use brainstorming to generate possible solutions. Try to make up a list of as many possible solutions as you can both come up with. Then, try to reduce it to a Plan A and Plan B. Try one plan and see what you learn from the experience. Make a commitment pact between you, promising to take responsibility to make changes. Try to make an honest effort — you might be pleasantly surprised. Remember, there is no failure. We learn from every experience.

Problem solving rather than blaming!

Additional Issues in Couple Therapy

My education and training also involved taking courses in sex therapy. Very often, **sexual issues** were central to the problems between partners. Having already established a working relationship with my clients, it was often easier for them to discuss sexual problems. Treatment involved relaxation and desensitization techniques. Sexual functioning options, such as exploring fantasy, sexual play, new positions, or sexual stimulation activities, were also suggested.

Scripts and habits from previous relationships, whether marriage or dating, can cause major issues in current relationships. Unresolved problems, acquired expectations, and habits will play out as before unless effort is made to change ways of thinking and behaving. Having been hurt by a previous partner can sometimes cause an apprehension that your new partner may hurt you as well.

Scripts and habits also refer to roles when reaching the living-together stage. For example, who cooks, cleans the bathroom, shops, or does the laundry. Important issues like spending and controlling money and planning events need to be agreed upon openly. I frequently heard comments like, "I'm not your parent or servant," or "Don't tell me what to do," and "It's my money, not yours." Adult-based couples work out compromises, while some couples continue the same old Child-Parent conflict.

Courtship in a new relationship often starts with a period of mutual admiration. Love is blind. In a new courting relationship, we put our best foot forward to impress each other. "Hey, look at me! I am the one you want." We usually watch our behavior and hold back on bad habits and unpleasant attitudes. We show respect and attention to the needs, interests, and desires of our partner. We go the extra mile to do the little things that matter most. We bring flowers, listen attentively, dress upscale, and watch our hygiene.

As a relationship moves to a longer-term state, our bad habits begin to surface. We might start to treat our partners in the same destructive manner as we did in the last unsuccessful relationship. Some individuals have been treated badly in prior relationships and have learned to expect the same mistreatment. It can become a self-fulfilling, destructive, reoccurring path. Defensiveness increases and counter-defenses go up. These are important exposed nerves to address. We cannot let the damaged past ruin a promising future.

It is particularly important to openly agree upon a new working contract and a promise to be considerate of each other's needs, interests, and desires. We need to be mindful that we could be slipping into taking our partner for granted. One of the greatest problems I have noticed with couples is when they stop courting each other. When courting, we share interests and look forward to spending time with our partner. We should never forget courtship.

When I find myself slipping, I have learned to put a 3x5 card on my vanity mirror with one word: **Courtship.** Hanging up a post card is a great way to remind ourselves to right the course.

Let courtship guide the relationship!

Anxiety and Depression

Considerable attention to adult treatment issues has already been given in sections pertaining to parenting, relationships, enhancing life experiences, understanding OCD, and forgiveness. Please review these previous sections. My work also focused on adult issues of anxiety and depression. In the following sections, I will include additional insights and perspectives on these topics.

Whether I was addressing anxiety or depression, a careful assessment was made at intake to consider a wide array of variables that could be impacting the problem. As I pointed out earlier, taking time to examine many factors will help to avoid overlooking an important contributor. Getting a clear picture of any **biological factors** is key when treating anxiety and depression. Clients need a good medical work-up to rule out possible metabolic causes of mood disorders, such as hormonal imbalances, vitamin deficiencies, and serious health problems, like cardio-vascular issues. Some of these conditions require medication alongside psychological and behavioral treatment.

With all my clients, I engaged in an educational treatment strategy. In addressing anxiety and depression, I taught everyone about How We Make a Feeling, The Experience and Failure Roads, as well as the CPA concepts: Child, Parent, and Adult. These important concepts formed a basis for treatment and for teaching self-help.

Anxiety issues often involved phobias, procrastination, poor social confidence, panic attacks, and obsessive-compulsive disorder. Following cognitive training, my focus shifted to teaching relaxation skills. I liked to use the Jacobson (1938) relaxation program and variations of that approach of systematically relaxing muscle tension from head to toes. Additionally, my approach was influenced by learning and practicing yoga. I taught these skills and made tape recordings for home practice. Later, I referred to digital instructions found online.

I often employed variations of treatment approaches inspired by Dr. Joseph Wolpe's (1969) systematic desensitization model. This model uses cognitive-behavioral skills, relaxation, and gradual exposure to the phobic situation either *in vitro* or *in vivo*. Clients were helped to construct a hierarchy for approaching a target from a least-anxious state to an intensified, anxious state. A scale of 1 to 10 was created to approximate the level of anxious feelings, called SUDs, or "subjective units of discomfort," with 10 being the worst possible feelings. Clients were instructed to imagine, while remaining calm, a low-level image that evoked a certain level SUD. With effort, they could begin to progressively imagine more and more anxiety-provoking images until they no longer scored high SUDs.

While practicing visualizations of approaching the actual, fear-provoking event, clients also practiced in real-time the actual behavior of approaching the fearful situations. I gave an account of this approach in Volume One with my example of helping a child with a bee phobia (see "Treating Anxiety: Phobias and OCD).

I have used the same model with adults for elevator and other height phobias, and with issues such as driving on highways or crossing bridges. The model was also used with animal phobias as well as social phobias.

Depression issues also involved overcoming considerable Failure Road thinking. Overreacting negatively led to a fixation on feelings of guilt and hopelessness. The "light at the end of the tunnel" seemed to be beyond their reach. Many of my depressed clients exhibited poor self-esteem and a lack of significant interests and passions. It was also noted that many had poor social skills, lived socially isolated lives, and had many anxiety issues as well.

For these clients, it was very important to establish a trusting relationship early in the treatment. There was a strong need for a sense of safety and security. Many of my clients had a significant history of hurtful experiences. Once this sense of trust was established, then they could entertain learning Experience Road, Adult stage thinking. Trust seemed to be tested often. These clients were well practiced in living fearful of abandonment.

Panic Attacks

Over time I saw many clients with **panic anxiety attacks**. Some of these clients had attacks while driving, shopping, or prior to public speaking or social engagements. Some also had panic attacks in public restrooms which inhibited urination. People with panic attacks get an intense rush of adrenaline entering their blood stream. Their breathing becomes exceedingly difficult, their heart races as if their chest will explode, and they sweat excessively. They can potentially pass out. Again, it is important to get a good medical screening as there are some medical conditions that produce panic attacks.

My behavioral treatment for panic attacks involved teaching an in-depth understanding of the fight-or-flight response. As previously discussed, when it is an over-reaction to a false alarm, it can endanger our lives. We can rush foolishly into danger zones and attack others who may not pose a real threat to us, as well as place ourselves in more dangerous situations.

To highlight how quickly this reaction occurs, I sometimes surprised my clients by rushing forward and screaming at them. They immediately experienced the fight-or-flight response. Afterwards, I apologized profusely while they calmed down.

This sudden rush of adrenaline can be an extremely uncomfortable experience. People who have panic attacks often believe they are going to die. In turn, this fear can trigger an increase in the fight-or-flight response, producing more adrenaline and prolonging the attack. Following a panic attack, there can be a period of extreme exhaustion due to having expended an intense amount of energy.

There are also people who get random, false-alarm panic attacks without any history of trauma or current eliciting stimulus. Somewhere in their nervous system they have a faulty circuit that can cause this glitch. The sudden attack often results in the same panic of impending demise, and they get stuck in the same loop with extreme adrenaline reactions.

The treatment involves stopping the adrenaline reaction of panicking and letting the adrenaline rush run its course. It may take ten minutes for the sensations of an adrenaline rush to subside if no further alarms are triggered. If one does not continue with more "Oh, my god! I am going to die!" thoughts, then no additional adrenaline will be pumped into their bloodstream.

My clients were given a clear understanding of this mechanism. They underwent relaxation and breathing skill training. They were taught not to run away when this happens but to calmly step to the side or to a nearby Safety Zone and begin coping skills. The first skill is to start slowing down breathing. Remember, as muscles tense up and our heart races, the brain receives less oxygen from the bloodstream. Reasoning cannot occur if the brain is in a state of alarm.

A hierarchy of panic-inducing situations was developed, followed by practice through visualization and, later, with real-life situations. They visualized they were feeling the panic and then saw themselves begin to breathe while focusing on a calming image. A buzz word was used to elicit the calming or "safe" image. As I mentioned earlier, I use "Tennessee" as my buzz word, which quickly brings my awareness to a mountain scene.

It is particularly important to address the fear of dying. A more rational understanding about life and death needs to be developed, such as the "white blood cells vs. viruses" concept I addressed previously.

Clients who had panic attacks while driving were taught to pull over to the side of the road, park the car, roll down the window, turn off the car, and tell themselves, "Ok, body. Finish your adrenaline rush. I'll wait patiently." They would turn on the radio or open a newspaper or just gaze at the world around them while reassuring themselves that it was alright. As they gained confidence in controlling the adrenaline rush, attacks became less frequent, shorter, and less severe. The panic attack was also used as a signal to take a better look at their own personal stress levels. They reminded themselves to be more aware of taking time to bring down stress levels throughout their daily lives. They practiced mindfulness stress-reduction skills throughout the day.

Humor is an excellent way to distract oneself from prolonged focusing on panic images. A good joke or funny picture can go a long way in reducing tension. Laughter is a natural remedy. Life can get stressful, but sometimes we must step back and find our humorous WOW. The following example illustrates using humor during a panic attack.

A client of mine would have panic attacks while at the supermarket. I helped her to visualize falling into a large display of canned soup. Soup would then spill out from the cans, making the floor slippery and causing people to bump into each other and fall as well. Soon everyone was falling and knocking over more displays. Then they'd start to fall out the door into the street, causing passersby to fall over into a human chain, on and on like dominoes. Picturing the absurdity of this was eventually comical. The focus was to exaggerate the issue and take it to an impossible conclusion.

I have also used a similar script with people who worked themselves into a panic attack, such as people obsessed about getting sick and vomiting at school or in a store. They often avoided going into stores, to work, or to school. I will spare you the image of my script and leave it to your own imagination. This approach is similar to the advice given to people with a fear of public speaking — to picture their audience in their underwear. Indeed, good speakers always seem to start with a funny story. Everyone laughs and relaxes. Even in the great musical, *The King and I*, the young children are taught to whistle a happy tune whenever they feel afraid. Others often pray when frightened. Whatever can keep one from not focusing on panicky thoughts will help keep the mind under control and defuse the fight-or-flight reaction.

Over time, as my clients gained control over their fears, they also gained confidence to go on with life. If they felt panic, they would quickly switch into coping skills, knowing they would be fine shortly. We all feel anxious at times, but, with a healthier outlook on life and good coping skills, we can stay on the Experience Road and face our destinies.

***A calming breath, a sense of humor, and a positive attitude
can take us a long way on the Experience Road!***

Obsessive-compulsive Disorder (OCD)

In Volume One, I gave an extensive account of **The Gatekeeper** biological foundation of OCD. Please review that section (see "Treating Anxiety: Phobias and OCD"). OCD with adults presented significant challenges due to their many years of prolonged, inappropriate behavior. As I have mentioned before, this problem, from my experiences, cannot be treated from a reasoning perspective. My clients knew their behavior was irrational. The desire to do the compulsion or to obsess had a strong grip on their lives. The ability to hold back or avoid committing the act was very weak. Periods of high levels of stress often exacerbated OCD. Learning to live a less stressful life was a major component of treatment. The worlds of my OCD patients were often extremely complicated.

With many of my clients, a combined treatment involving medication and behavior therapy was used. It was also necessary to have frequent sessions early in treatment, then gradually space sessions out over the course of treatment.

It was essential to get my clients to understand the biological aspects of The Gatekeeper OCD model I previously presented. The obsessive-compulsive behavior is tied into specific, inborn neurological systems. Each of us is born with certain levels of stress that our nervous systems can process. Some people can withstand considerable degrees of stress without any adverse reactions. They can perform amazing feats of endurance under difficult conditions. They can ski down a mountain slope, do a triple loop, and land on their feet, smiling. On the opposite end of the spectrum are individuals who have considerable difficulty handling minimal levels of stress. They quickly become overwhelmed and make poor decisions. Most of us fall somewhere in the middle.

Our ability to handle stress can be enhanced or diminished by our experiences. Those individuals on the Experience Road find strength from what they have gone through, while those on the Failure Road become more limited and dysfunctional. All of us, according to our inborn nature, will exhibit or experience stress in different ways. Some will get somatic symptoms, such as stomach pain or headaches. Others will become withdrawn or angry. Still, others will perform rituals and become obsessed beyond that which can be easily handled rationally, as with OCD.

Early life experiences, as I explained in Volume One, can leave a **stain** on the nervous system due to trauma. This stain becomes a negative influence on how we interpret sensory information coming into our nervous system. We can never remove this stain through reasoning, but we can become aware of how it is impacting our judgment and then counter that influence in the current moment. We all have gatekeepers throughout our nervous systems whose function is to decide whether the information passing through is important enough to keep passing along until it gets the attention of our BOSS in the brain. This process is so fast that we are often unaware of its influence. Gatekeepers are natural and can be influenced by trauma. They can quickly react to save our lives or overreact to a false alarm, placing us in more danger.

With OCD, a breakdown in The Gatekeeper system continues to signal danger and places too much importance on irrelevant information. The result is that some people get stuck in a loop of obsessions and compulsions. The information is misinterpreted, the alarm goes off, and the behavior is the reaction. **They need to know they are not choosing to be a bad person, rather it is a breakdown of the biological Gatekeeper system that is responsible for their behavior.** Knowing this can often alleviate guilt, lessen anxiety, and provide new strength to work through counter-conditioning programs. There is, to date, no specific medication that stops OCD. Medication is used to calm the nervous system in hopes it can make controlling OCD somewhat easier.

My patients were taught to recognize when the alarm had gone off and to evaluate whether it was real or false. Their behavior or bodily sensations could become signals that said, "Oops, I'm doing it again!" They are then taught to become the gatekeeper and to manually shut off the alarm. Combining relaxation therapy and cognitive behavioral skills, they could, with considerable practice, gain control over the defective gatekeeper.

In combination with learning to become the gatekeeper, gradual exposure methods of systematic desensitization as well as thought-stopping skills were also taught. Learning to develop new coping strategies for stress reduction is also especially important. Knowing when a SUD level is rising and then engaging in a stress-reduction activity is critical. If we can keep our SUD level lower, we gain more power to become the gatekeeper. If we walk around with a high-level SUD and a security gatekeeper is triggered, those with OCD will have less ability to gain control or become the gatekeeper.

Overcoming OCD is a lifelong process. It can be a debilitating problem that consumes one's life. My clients required considerable years of help to gain control after the many years they engaged in OCD activity. Refresher periods of therapy were needed throughout their lives. Those of my clients who clearly accepted The Gatekeeper concept made better progress, while those who still searched for the underlying, traumatic event to explain their OCD made less.

Become your gatekeeper!

Hoarding

Later in my years of practice, I began working with the problem of hoarding. This is an extreme, OCD set of behaviors that can become life-crippling. The adult clients I saw were overwhelmed with troubling emotions. They came to therapy searching for the one underlying, psycho-dynamic event that could explain their behavior. They believed that, if they could find that event, it would release them from years of guilt and anxiety. They lived in homes filled with unnecessary clutter stored up over a lifetime. Most of my hoarding clients were experiencing severe stress with their life partners as a result of the hoarding.

These clients were usually bright people who were still gainfully employed. They had been in steady, lengthy relationships. Their partners were also emotionally exhausted but remained loyal to their suffering partner. There were some partners who were also clutter bugs.

My clients had an extensive history of unsuccessful treatment, from psychotherapy to medication trials. By the time they arrived in my office, they were depressed and, at times, even suicidal. They appeared to have lost touch with any passions or hope.

My treatment approach was to teach skill development and an understanding of the interaction of biological factors. The client and their significant other, if possible, were both required to attend sessions. As I have explained in previous sections (Volume One section "Treating Anxiety: Phobias and OCD" and Volume Two section "Obsessive-compulsive Disorder (OCD)"), OCD is based in biology. OCD does not respond to reasoning and psycho-dynamic approaches. OCD/Hoarding behavior is related to **The Gatekeeper** concept I presented previously. Please review those sections.

It is extremely important to understand that hoarding behavior is due to faulty gatekeepers. It is not the hoarder's fault. They are not bad people, punishing themselves due to some unconscious psycho-dynamic event. Their behavior is stuck in a loop. They cannot filter out important from unimportant messages; every event is given the same serious assessment or designation. Their brain's **BOSS** desk becomes flooded with every minor detail as if it was urgent. Every event becomes **HAT**. This assessment triggers the **fight-or-flight** response, pumping unnecessary amounts of adrenaline into their system. This results in the brain getting less oxygen, leading to less brain power to do problem solving. Their lives are in a constant state of emergency. They can only focus on the simple decision to retain objects rather than discard them. "What should I do? I do not know. Ok, hold on to it until I figure it out." Avoiding the problem is the solution they accept.

Medication treatments provided some relief from anxiety but do not correct the gatekeeper's malfunctioning. It is especially important to accept that this gatekeeper problem will be a lifelong coping issue. My clients had never heard their problem explained with respect to gatekeepers. For them, this concept was like opening a well of relief. They had a way to understand that took away the guilt and endless search for the underlying psycho-dynamic problem. It was not because their parents did not love them. They began to see that, perhaps, they could learn to close the gate and make a more constructive decision.

"I am the gatekeeper" became their new mantra. They were taught to recognize the body message that the gate was left open to the BOSS. They learned to accept this and to ask themselves a problem-solving question such as, "Do I really need to keep this?"

This concept worked well with mild to moderate hoarders. Clients who had years of intense hoarding had a difficult time mastering this new concept and skill. For these clients, I developed the concept of the **Prosthetic Gatekeeper**. A prosthetic is a device that can be used to supplement a person's functioning when a biological part of the body cannot be used. A pacemaker can help a weak heart. A person can get a prosthetic arm, hand, or leg. Someone can use a wheelchair to get around, get glasses to improve vision, or procure a hearing aid to help hearing. These devices are externally or internally attached to help the person function. There are many adjustment devices that can be modified to give a person with physical impairments a greater range to their quality of life.

In the case of my extreme hoarders, there was often a life partner or family member who could become a Prosthetic Gatekeeper. They could make the decisions to resolve collection issues. If the hoarder could be helped to accept the nature of their personal gatekeeper biology, then they could more easily accept the assistance of the caring helper. They needed to understand and accept that an external Prosthetic Gatekeeper was just like a wheelchair for someone whose body does not allow them to walk.

With the life partner or family member engaged in the treatment, the partner could resolve their own angst. They could, without feeling guilty or wasting time with the futile practice of reasoning with the hoarder, make constructive and swift decisions. The hoarder was also encouraged to find their WOW and engage in previous or new passions. This was especially important to the treatment. Given the years of strongly ingrained, habitual behavior, a hoarder will struggle in letting go of the collected mess. Learning relaxation skills and engaging with appropriate hobbies serve to distract them as they work to control anxiety levels brought on from making changes. The Prosthetic

Gatekeeper serves as co-therapist to remind their loved one of The Gatekeeper concept. The couple and family are also encouraged to improve their relations and share in hobbies and passions. At times, the Prosthetic Gatekeeper has to call in other types of Prosthetic Gatekeepers, such as weekly cleaning services and even household junk removers.

Initially during treatment, the hoarder will need frequent sessions then, later, spaced or extended sessions to help reinforce The Gatekeeper concept. This concept is a simple and easy way to understand hoarding. Even if earlier childhood events have left a stain on the nervous system, reasoning will not remove the stain. Learning how to live with gatekeeper deficiencies is more productive.

Hoarding is a form of OCD. It is based in biology.
Learn to become the gatekeeper or accept a Prosthetic Gatekeeper.

Social Anxiety

Over my professional years I have seen many clients with social anxiety problems. It was exceedingly difficult for them to develop friendships, talk in public, and have general conversations. It is important to note that skill differences naturally vary among people. There are individuals who are extremely talented with certain skills such as those seen in sports, arts, music, and public speaking. At the other extreme are people with significant, limited skills or talents. Most people fall into the average skill range and can contribute meaningfully to an activity, but not at the highest levels. For example, I love sports and music, yet even with extensive training, I will never be able to hit a homerun in Yankee Stadium or achieve a symphony-concert level of music presentation.

Within the social-skills domain, there are two extremes that have been used to describe and differentiate between the personalities of individuals: the introversion and extroversion personality concept. People who fall into the introvert camp tend to be quiet or passive, more introspective, move in smaller social circles, and prefer a quieter, steadier way of life. The extrovert enjoys a busier lifestyle experience, likes to be noticed, makes conversations easily, makes many friendships, and is seen as outgoing and gregarious.

It was once thought that the extrovert personality was more acceptable and positive than the introvert personality. Introversion was considered undesirable — a negative personality trait that hung over the heads of quieter people. Those who, by nature, preferred a quieter lifestyle were left to feel that something must be wrong with them. Over my many years in treating clients,

I found this dichotomy to be ridiculous. People vary with social lifestyle as much as with other talents I previously mentioned.

Most of us fall within the average range with a mixed bag of social skills. Being an individual at either extreme may just be a natural reflection of your inborn nature. For instance, my friend Tom could walk into a room and, within minutes, he was able to strike up conversations, promote humor, and everyone knew his name. It just came easy for him. I, as well as others, took more time to engage or ease into the social flow of a room full of people.

Having an introverted personality is one of many normal states of human nature. It is no better or worse than having an extroverted personality, and vice versa. It is ok for some people to be quieter individuals — no guilt necessary.

We are all a mixed bag of skills and abilities!

It was important to understand this issue when I met people who wanted to improve their social skills. Adding some conversations skills, for example, might help with relationships — personal or otherwise. There were also clients whose social skills were greatly affected by social anxiety. I will address my work with that group.

A major contributor to social anxiety is, again, an issue of which **road of life** philosophy one adheres to. Often, socially anxious people tend to follow the Failure Road of life. They are too consumed with the fear of rejection. Not being able to please everyone makes them feel like a reject. It is safer to avoid social engagement than risk loss of approval. Learning to switch over to the Experience Road was the first direction I advised. Remember that, on the Experience Road, failure and rejection do not exist. It is accepted that you cannot please everyone, and not everyone will be your friend no matter how nice you try to be.

Socially anxious clients still had deficits with certain skills. One target area is to get to **know yourself**. What do you like? What are your opinions and preferences? What turns you on? What is it that brings you WOW? There are some things we naturally enjoy as well as some things that are not naturally exciting to us. Considerable time was spent exploring their **passions.** With some individuals, it was important to get them to try out potential new passions, like taking a camera and going on a nature hike, trying a style of food they never tried before, listening to a lecture, or seeing a different style of movie.

It was important to discover their personal preferences and opinions. It could simply be what scent of deodorant they enjoyed, or their favorite color, breakfast cereal, fast food, music, etc. They could try listening to the news and forming an opinion.

At this stage of my work it was important to help someone become their **own best friend**. Give up trying to figure out what everyone else likes and focus on what you like. When you have interests and opinions, you have something to bring to conversations. Being your own best friend means going places, even by yourself, to enjoy that event for your own pleasure. So many people cannot go to a movie alone out of fear of what it looks like to others to be seen alone. A movie is a personal experience. No one tells you to laugh, cry, or scream out in surprise. Your reaction is your own. Later, you can talk about how you felt about the movie rather than whom you went with. This was a common homework assignment I gave out.

Check your life road, gain passions, and be kind to yourself!

Overcoming social anxiety means not being afraid to be **noticed**. So many of my clients lived in a world of being afraid to be seen. It was important to eliminate this fear. They were given homework assignments, such as wearing two different shoes to class or work, or wearing a silly hat, shirt, or a pin with a cute saying. They had to see that nothing HAT would happen if they were noticed in a different way.

Developing conversation skills involves many steps. In the first step, it is important to become more **spontaneous.** Some of my techniques were previously presented in the Volume One section "Social-Skills Group Therapy for Children." Please take a moment to review that section. I used word association games and silly acting drills. Conversations were held speaking only gibberish. I had to model these activities. One of my favorite activities involved taking an object and bringing it to life. I called these "animisms." What would an object say or feel if it could talk? For example, what if you were a chair and a very heavy person sat on you, or if you were an apple and found a worm crawling inside of you? We would go back and forth, challenging each other to take an object and be spontaneous. Laughing at oneself is relieving!

Within conversations, it is also important to acknowledge **emotional** messages. Drills using nonsense words were used to express and convey feelings. In a give-and-take conversation, the emotional messages through voice and body language are 90% of the conversation. One can take a simple phrase, such as "I love you," and change its meaning just by the way it is expressed. We worked on eye contact as well, holding staring contests to break through the fear of being seen or looking at someone. We also practiced giving compliments.

Practicing conversations is critical. Learning to start a conversation can be challenging. I taught people to **survey** the person and situation. Look at the person and notice them: what are they wearing? Jewelry? An unusual color or pattern of clothing? A hat? Can you give them a compliment? Are they carrying a book or listening to music? What is the common situation? Are you both in the same class, restaurant, store, etc.? All these immediate sources of information can be used to start a conversation.

Try bringing up a **topic** such as your favorite sports team, TV show, music group, or video game. Avoid politics and religion initially. See if there is anything you have in common. In a conversation, remember not to dominate, but acknowledge what you hear before changing topics. "Wow, it seems you really like soccer. Tell me more about your favorite player." Stay on the topic for a few back-and-forth, give-and-take comments. When there is a pause, then ask about music. Start with offering your interest in music, then ask them if they have an interest in this topic.

We practiced extensively until we maintained good eye contact, demonstrated emotional language, revealed preferences and points of view, and the conversation flowed smoothly without sounding robotic or rehearsed.

Above all, it is important to smile. Do not be afraid to be noticed. If the conversation goes nowhere, see what you have learned and give yourself positive reinforcement. Praise yourself for trying.

In addition to conversation training, a hierarchy of socially-anxious situations would be constructed, and homework assignments were drawn from the list. It could be ordering a slice of pizza, dining alone, shopping for a shirt and then returning it the next day, asking for directions, going to the movies alone, sitting at a table with others in the dining hall at college or work, saying hello to random strangers at work or school, etc. The last achievement was to join an organization of people reflective of their interest or hobby. As a way of making friends, clients also tried volunteering to help with an activity.

Social skills can be developed. Be willing to learn!

PTSD: Post-traumatic Stress Disorder

A mom stands on her front porch and watches the hurricane's flood waters rising, worrying about getting her children to safety. Her home was severely damaged. Months later, she cannot sleep and is crying constantly. Her marriage is crumbling, and she can no longer drive on roadways within a few miles of waterways.

There is a very bright and skilled man a few years way from retirement who has worked for thirty years in the same company. He is anticipating his pension when the company suddenly closes and goes bankrupt. There is no pension. The man's marriage is failing, and he has spent the last year depressed, out of work, drinking, and gambling.

A woman is driving in her car when she is suddenly rear-ended in a car accident. Months later she is extremely anxious, stops driving, loses her job, and withdraws from social interests and friends.

There is a commanding officer whose job is to assemble his soldiers to deploy to a war zone. He also must arrange for handling deceased soldiers while, at the same time, actively working to recruit replacements. He had experienced mortar fire in Iraq while on an inspection tour over a year ago. He is now a year away from retirement. He is seriously depressed, afraid of loud noises, and withdrawing from family and friends.

What did these clients of mine have in common? They had **post-traumatic stress disorder or PTSD.** Most of us tend to think of soldiers returning from active duty when we hear PTSD. The media has clearly made the public aware of the plight of military personnel. It has been well documented. My other clients' experiences, however, were also traumatic. Events occurred that challenged the foundation of the lifelong beliefs that have held them together. Such events do not often make the news headlines. They can often be overlooked but can still result in PTSD. For my clients, nothing was making sense anymore.

What else do they have in common? Their lives and those of their loved ones were falling apart. They did not understand why. They were trying to lock up their feelings, but the containment walls were crumbling. When events are traumatic, we tend to want to bury or block those feelings out of our awareness. As I mentioned previously with the circle of emotional energy demonstration (see the "Forgiveness" section), we construct an emotional strongbox in the center of our emotional life. As time goes on, the feelings and memories try to surface. Often our reaction is to place more energy into reinforcing the walls to contain those experiences. Over time, less energy is available for current emotional experiences.

I have seen a pattern that occurs at the time of traumatic impact. The first response many of my clients made in the first moments of the trauma was to shout, "Oh, my God!" They were not necessarily religious comments, but more of a statement that the support for their existence has suddenly disappeared. As I mentioned in Volume One regarding the Age of Discovery child, our most basic human needs are **biology and security**.

We are raised early in life to believe that someone or something will provide us security, keeping us safe. There will be parents and family, friends, teachers, police, government, religious institutions, and bosses — someone to catch us when we fall. We become dependent upon having somebody or something to have our backs in crisis times. Many of my clients, like most people, were raised to believe that God has their back. Some of my clients asked or cried out, "Why has God failed me?" "I am one of the good guys!" "Why am I being punished?" "What did I do wrong?"

Others in times of crisis seem to pick themselves up and find a way to stay in control and manage their way through it. Why do some people seem to cope better with trauma while others cannot? I have found that the answer often reflects the concept of **internal vs. external locus of control**: what controls me, versus what do I control?

People with an **internal** sense of control adopt a way of making sense of life's trials and tribulations from a more rational point of view. They are more often grounded in a scientific or factual understanding of events and experiences. They are raised, in times of trouble, to investigate their own strengths as a basis for having their own backs. They give themselves security. They often have accepted their mortality, knowing that someday and some place they will die. They embrace the Experience Road point of view, learning as they go along and not fearing the great unknown. Their lives are more grounded in Adult thinking.

People with an internal sense of control stay more in touch with their emotions. They will talk about events and draw strength from their experiences. They have learned to pick themselves up. Their lives are centered on FAD ways of reacting. There is no need for an emotional strongbox to hide their feelings in. More of their emotional energy can go into problem solving.

People with an **external** sense of control are those who, more often, expect someone or something to take care of them. They often lack skills or confidence to have their own backs. Self-confidence and self-doubt issues can arise. They live more within the framework of the Failure Road philosophy. The unknown and dying are more unsettling. A HAT reaction to difficult moments is more common throughout their lives. When events go badly, they do not look to their own strengths to do problem solving. They do not want to talk about it. They may cry and complain, but they believe talking about it will only make it worse. There is often a Child/Parent maturity issue.

Interestingly, many people with an external locus, in a time of crisis, can find a way to get out of harm's way. Yet, in the end, they still perceive their rescue to be from divine providence or external support. Indeed, they may have luckily been saved by someone, but they will eventually break down emotionally and become overwhelmed with fear, anxiety, or depression. The fear that, if someone had not come along, they would have died, cripples them into withdrawing from living life and taking risks. They want guarantees they will be safe.

Coping with PTSD requires learning to talk about the events. It is especially important not to let the person develop that emotional strongbox, hiding away the experience and feelings. No matter how long it takes, they need to keep talking. They can draw, sing, or write, but they must keep expressing. Emotional energy needs to go into growth, not suppression.

At the same time, it is necessary to explore exposed nerves developed in childhood and to work hard to gain Adult, Experience Road perspectives. It takes considerable courage and effort to overcome PTSD. If a person is aware of what they are facing and understands the concepts of coping, they may have an easier time of managing things should they regress.

Does your sense of security depend on an internal or external locus of control?

Adult ADHD and Uncluttering Your Home and Workplace.

Please review the Volume One section "Perspectives on ADHD" (for children). In addition to children, I have also worked with many adults who had ADHD. Again, this condition is based in biology. The causes can be multifaceted biological problems. Contrary to early beliefs, ADHD does not go away with adulthood; it lasts a lifetime. Over the course of years, many adults figure out ways to cope with this condition. The clients I treated had a poor understanding of ADHD and never adjusted well to this problem. These individuals struggled as children in school and continued to struggle with work. They were disorganized, forgetful, and very inconsistent with job requirements. Emotionally, they were often depressed. They had poor self-images with low self-confidence and frequently struggled with social relationships.

After careful assessment to ascertain that the ADHD had, indeed, been present during their formative years, these clients felt an immediate sense of relief. They finally understood this aspect of their personality. They had been blaming themselves for years and feeling inadequate for the difficulties they faced each day. As their homes became more out of control, their environment became more cluttered, almost resembling that of hoarders. I did find a difference related to gatekeepers. Clients with ADHD seemed to have less of a problem with gatekeepers. With instruction and understanding, they learned skills to manage their ADHD. The hoarders struggled greatly with skill-acquisition and gaining control.

With effort, these clients could learn organizational skills, develop better anger management skills, and improve social skills. Just like with children, they had to learn how to break down a task, find the entry path, and step back to a Safety Zone to regain focus when necessary.

Where to begin a task was a major problem. I remember two teenagers I had in group therapy whose behaviors highlighted this issue. Both were seventeen years old, bright, creative, and diagnosed with ADHD. Teen 1 had just learned he was accepted to college and was in full panic mode. He was overwhelmed with thoughts of the seemingly insurmountable task of getting through college. He had no sense of where to begin this journey. Teen 2 was a budding international chess star. Chess is an extraordinarily complex activity that requires concentration and planning. I asked Teen 2 how he managed to play so well considering his ADHD. His response was that he studied how great players began their games. Once he knew how to begin, he could follow a plan.

Teen 1 was taught to break each day down into manageable tasks. Make a schedule, record notes, go home, have dinner, relax, and then find a distraction-free place to transcribe notes, place important dates on a calendar, and color code what and when assignments were due. The goal was to take each day one day at a time. He began to see the path. He eventually graduated in four years.

I applied this same method to help a young man improve his job performance. He was working in a supermarket and was in danger of losing his job due to inconsistent work performance. He was responsible for stocking two aisles as well as retrieving items from the storeroom to fill call-in orders. He was totally lost. His section was disheveled and missing products.

The first step was where to begin: He was instructed to stand at one edge of a row and, with his arms shoulder length apart, scan the three levels of shelves, starting at the top and working his way down, and record on his phone what items were needed. He was to repeat this step continuously until he had gone through the whole aisle. He quickly improved keeping his area straight and well stocked.

He was also asked to go into the storeroom and create a map of where items were stocked. Once the map reflected a clear path of where to find items, he would stand at the front of the storeroom and use his map as a pathfinder. He also hung up his map at home, where he could study it. His work improved greatly.

I have included a handout explaining the concepts and approaches I employed to treat this issue. Please refer to the handout "The Management of Adult Attention-deficit/Hyperactivity Disorder: Uncluttering Your Home and Workplace" in the Appendix on Page 186 for specific information.

> ***It is possible to learn skills to improve life functioning rather than let ADHD become a lifetime burden!***

Summary

The journey of the Experience Road has led me to this point: to document my experiences. As I look back, I am overwhelmed by how much I have learned and contributed to the lives of others. This has also been a journey of personal growth. I shared with my clients and have led by example.

Over the course of this book, I have attempted to cover a vast array of issues relative to children and adults, I have tried to put forth an understanding of my own unique methods and perspectives of treatment. I do not dare claim that everything I have presented is original, but I do believe that, like any artist, one takes the palette and creates their own impressions and interpretations.

I am proud of my concepts of a teaching model to treatment as well as the perspectives of the Experience vs. Failure Roads of life. These concepts were my foundations. I hope the knowledge I acquired can be passed on to others. There is ample material for self-help and guidance for children, families, and adults. I also believe that my concepts can help other mental health providers have a model that can guide their own professional practices.

As with any book, it is not a substitute for working with a therapist. My book has attempted to give focus and direction to assist in the resolution of problems.

I am not sure where the Experience Road will take me, but I feel more confident knowing that I have these memories written down, and I can carry them with me, ready to be referred to as needed. I genuinely enjoyed writing this book and hope the reader has found my material helpful in whatever manner they chose.

In the Appendix, I have included handouts, worksheets, and signs that I regularly gave out to my clients.

Appendix

Family as a Country — Case Study: Chris

There was a period of ten years where I was a regular guest presenter at a local high school psychology class. My topic was behavioral intervention, and I would present the following case study of a boy named Chris to demonstrate the **Family as Country** concept.

I worked with Chris when he was eight years old. He had two siblings and both parents. Family life was constant fighting, both verbally and physically. Chris also had problems in school with academics and social relationships.

Using the Family as a Country model, I examined each level to assess and prescribe interventions. As mentioned previously, I would work with each level through different modalities to teach skills and address issues in order to have a comprehensive treatment approach.

The Government: Needs of the Parents

Assessment: His parents were married, middle class, and working often on different shifts. They had graduated high school and had some college credits. They described themselves as incredibly stressed out. Chris was the oldest child and out of control, while the younger siblings were beginning to model their brother. The parents fought frequently with each other as well as with Chris.

The parents had different approaches to parenting, based on their upbringing. The mother was from a family that yelled and threatened to punish the kids. To not repeat what her parents had done, she often tried to reason with Chris. Eventually, this led her to lose her temper and give in to Chris's misbehavior. She often broke down into crying and blaming herself for being a poor mother.

The father's approach was to detach and withdraw from the kids. He would work and expect his wife to handle the home life. He rarely played with Chris, throwing up his hands and saying, "This kid is too different from me." He seemed to relate somewhat better to the younger siblings. When Chris acted up, the father would argue with the mother, blaming her for not controlling Chris. The father, in denial, also appeared to have a childhood of issues remarkably like his son's. He would have been diagnosed with ADHD and ODD, like Chris, had that been done when he was younger. The paternal grandparent also was distant from his son, the father.

The marriage was doing poorly and, as individuals, they seemed to not enjoy their lives very much. A sense of depression seemed to pervade the government/parents.

Treatment needs: Marital sessions to reconnect and develop parenting and communication/relationship skills. They needed to develop teamwork and to address personal needs, interests, and desires.

The Citizens: Needs of the Children

Assessment: As a child, Chris was easy to relate to. He seemed to be of at least average intelligence. He was highly attuned to his surroundings. Information suggested that Chris was also highly manipulative. He had once deliberately bruised his arm on the way to school in order to claim to the teachers that his parents had abused him. This was his reaction to being denied a privilege. He wanted to punish his parents. The school called CPS, and his parents got in trouble. The case was unfounded, but the result was to make his parents even more afraid of him. They were considering placing him in foster care.

Chris had been diagnosed with ADHD but was not on medication. He refused to help at home and would incite problems with his younger siblings. He was doing poorly at school, refusing to complete assignments. Socially, his peers avoided him. They would not include him for fear he would disrupt the activity. Chris was angry at his classmates.

I also diagnosed Chris as having oppositional defiant disorder. He was impulsive and distractible but not hyperactive.

Treatment needs: Chris required help with managing ADHD, learning skills for anger-frustration control, social-skill development, and positive emotional support for his self-esteem. He also required help to develop his learning skills.

The System of Law and Order

Assessment: The parents did not work as a team. Rules were inconsistently followed. The dominant approach to parenting was to argue, yell, or give in. The parents were intimidated by their son.

Treatment needs: Develop the Choose to Earn system. Eliminate reasoning and arguments.

The System of Love and Attention:

Assessment: The country was extremely oriented to discipline and lacking in balance. Chris acted out for attention or to punish his parents for lack of attention.

Treatment: Positive family time. Daily doses of finding positive, loving comments for everyone. Develop the father-son relationship. Strengthen the mother's resistance to rejection.

My **treatment plan** was designed to address the entire family/country. The **parents** needed **marital sessions** as well as **individual** sessions to address their needs. They had built up walls and harbored considerable anger. Each parent had some depression. The father needed to identify the similarities between his personality and nature and those of his son. He needed to develop empathy for Chris and stop projecting his childhood anger onto Chris. The mother needed to develop more self-confidence. **Parenting training** was essential.

Family sessions were held to learn how to play together, to introduce the Choose to Earn system, and for learning how to be positive. Father-son sessions were held to encourage more bonding. They needed to find common play activities.

Individual sessions for Chris involved learning anger/frustration-control skills and improving organization and learning skills. Individual sessions were also helpful to provide additional positive attention and to learn emotional-expressive skills.

Group social-skill sessions were employed to address deficits with social abilities. Group was also helpful in providing Chris with the experience of friendships.

School coordination was especially important in order to keep everyone on the same page. In addition, the parents needed to work closely with the school as a team. Communication between home and school was improved to address Chris's manipulations as well as his learning-skill deficits. Teachers also needed to offer additional support and helpful suggestions. I made frequent trips to visit teachers and maintained phone contact. A token economy was set up with points earned for daily effort. The points were used for rewards at home and for additional points that could be applied from the group-therapy token system.

Chris and his family spent two years in treatment. Progress was significant in all areas. Chris did not require medication. The marriage grew and Chris made friends and developed socially interactive interests. His self-esteem was greatly improved.

Street Games

I grew up in Queens, New York, in an era when kids played games in the streets of neighborhoods. Each block often had enough kids for two teams for any kind of game. You could always find someone to play with. We learned to cooperate and settle our own disagreements on the block. We were highly creative, and our imaginations fueled our fun. We would get up in the morning, have breakfast, and then our parents would tell us to go outside and play. They would remind us to be back for lunch or dinner as we sped away on our bikes. Older kids played with younger kids and would incorporate them into whatever games we made up. You could spontaneously knock on someone's door and ask if the child could come out and play — often, you were invited to come in and play.

It was a time when people sat on the stoops in front of their homes and did not hide behind high fences in backyards. Parents looked out for the kids on the block, offering snacks and beverages. Many times, a parent would get home early from work and either joined in the ongoing game or took a bunch of us to the park to set up a ball game.

We lived in an age without computers or video games, and with limited TV — if you were lucky enough to have a TV. No cell phones! Making a call from the family house phone was costly. So, when a parent wanted to contact their child, they would open the window, shout out their name and, like wildfire, the message was passed around child to child until it found him or her. "Michael, your mom is calling you." If you made it home within fifteen or twenty minutes, you were safe. Any later probably meant you were beyond your boundary safety-range and in trouble when you got home.

Parents did not obsessively worry. They believed in the kids' abilities to handle events. There would always be some problems. What has changed through the decades that has made parents worried is the media attention to problems and the 24/7, frightening news cycle. Studies have shown that the rates of pedophiles have remained constant over time. These days, parents believe a predator is lurking behind every tree. As a result, up went the backyard walls, playdates had to be scheduled, and every young child needed a cell phone.

Kids now play inside on mind-absorbing video games for endless hours. It would break my heart when I would ask the kids in my group sessions how many played outside over the weekend and no one would raise their hand. Too many parents were not playing with their kids, just letting them become absorbed by the screens.

I also found that kids were encouraged to have video playdates. At other times, kids were taken to pre-planned, controlled social events such as classes and lessons. Some of those activities were helpful for developing talents. On the other hand, the street games gave my generation unstructured time to learn to become self-sufficient. We organized our activities, solved problems such as making decisions over rules of play, settled differences by compromising, and chose what to do with boredom.

Boredom became the motivator for imagination and creativity. Having outside, face to face contact with other kids promoted considerable social-skill development. We learned to compromise, settle arguments by rock-paper-scissors, and supported each other in times of frustration. We learned a great deal about standing up to peer pressure. We also learned how to fight when necessary. Above all, we learned how to make real friendships.

On rainy days, we would find someone's basement and create variations of our street games. On snowy days, we frolicked in the snow all day, building forts, having snowball fights, and sledding. On hot days, we set up a sprinkler and played water street games. Summer camp was hanging out. We would make up a traveling sports team and challenge another block's kids to kickball, stickball, punch ball, tag, football, etc.

Within my social-skill therapy groups, I made it a point to recreate the spirit of street games. We would have a structured, learning-skill drill, such as how to make positive comments or handle frustrations, followed by a street game the group created. At times, we were able to go outside to the park across from my office. Other times, we just pushed back the furniture and rolled up the carpet. I am including a list of games with instructions. Games can be adapted for inside or outside use.

1. Stickball: When playing outside, there are two versions. The first style is played with or without pitching. Generally, a sewer cover-plate is designated as home plate. Using a modified broom handle or a specific stickball bat, a small rubber hand ball, such as a Spalding Pensie Pinkie, is to be hit as far as possible. The number of telephone poles it flies past on a fly designates a homer, triple, double, or single. If the ball is caught on a fly, the batter is out.

The second style is played with a wall with a strike zone painted on it. The batter stands in front of the wall and someone pitches from about forty to fifty feet away. Balls and strikes are counted. The distance a ball is hit determines the base total.

When playing inside, such as in an office, a strike zone should be delineated on a wall, like a bookcase, while someone pitches from ten feet away. Use a small plastic bat and a Nerf ball, sponge ball, a paper wad, or even a rolled-up sock. Designate areas to determine the type of hit. For example, hitting the back wall on a fly could be a homer.

2. Kickball or Punch ball: Variations of baseball can be set up by either kicking or punching a ball. The same rules for baseball count. In kickball, a larger type of ball is used, like a dodgeball or beach ball. A batter can be out if they are hit by a ball thrown by a defensive player while the batter is running the bases. If playing inside, always use a soft Nerf or beach ball type of ball.

3. Triangle ball: This game is styled after baseball but uses three bases in a triangle formation. I often played this in the park and used three trees. When playing in the street, it is played on a driveway with the opposing street curbs as bases. Often a large ball is used. The ball can be hit by hand or kicked as it is pitched. The object is to keep the ball on the ground within the triangle space. If kicked or hit on a fly beyond the boundary, then it is an out. It can only go beyond the boundary if it is a grounder. A fielder can cause an out by throwing the ball at a batter if they are not on the base, or throwing the ball at the tree before the batter arrives there. When playing inside, use a soft ball like a beach ball.

This game is extremely helpful in teaching impulsive kids to hold back and work on self-control. It also tends to equalize the competitive edge a more gifted player might have. The lesser-skilled child has a better chance to stay involved and finally enjoy a ball game.

4. Stoop ball: This game can be played solo or in teams. When playing outside, find a set of steps (stoop) in front of a yard or garden. Using a rubber ball or tennis ball, stand about five feet back and throw the ball at the stoop. If it hits right, the ball will ricochet. Sometimes it will fly over your head and, based on a predetermined distance, will reflect the type of base hit, such as a homer. If caught on a fly, it is an out. A ball hit on the ground can be an out if handled without an error — otherwise it is considered a single. When playing inside, find a board or inverted table and lean it against a wall. Using a soft type of ball, follow the same set of rules.

5. Wiffle Ball: A great driveway or backyard game. The game is played like baseball or stickball but uses a plastic bat and a plastic Wiffle ball.

6. Trash Can Basketball/Handball: This game can have many variations. Basically, use two wastepaper baskets placed at opposite ends. If played outside, a medium-sized ball is passed among one team while they try to throw it in the baskets. Defense can try to block, but cannot stand directly over the can. When playing inside, form smaller teams and use an exceptionally soft ball or rolled up ball of paper wrapped in tape. The basket can also be raised off the floor, according to what is available, to provide height.

Basketball games, such as **Around the World** or **Silly Shots,** can be played inside or outside. **Around the World,** when played outside, usually uses a standard-height hoop or even an adjustable-height hoop. A circle is created and, at various stops along the circle, a player must shoot and score a basket to continue going around the circle. If they miss, they then wait there while another child takes a turn. Play continues until someone has successfully made all the shots from every stop on the circle. This can be played inside using a variety of cans or hoops for a basket. **Silly Shots** is great for inside play. A child begins by taking any shot they wish. The others must take the same shot. If you miss, then it is a point against you. If you make the shot, then you can now take any silly shot you want, and the game continues. The focus is on being silly, such as imitating an animal taking the shot.

7. Handball: This game is an outside activity. There are two types: American and Chinese. In my old neighborhood, every school yard had a handball court. A rubber ball is hit with hands or paddles. American style is to hit the ball back to the wall without one bounce. With Chinese style, the ball is hit back to the wall on one bounce. There are spaces that are designated areas for each player. The lead player is the ace, then comes king, queen, etc. A player must hit a ball that bounces in their area or they move down the ladder and then try to move back up as other players fall back.

8. Catch a Fly is Up: This is another outside game. It can be played in two basic ways. The first way is for a batter to stand at a designated home plate and hit a ball in the air toward a group of kids. If someone can catch the ball on a fly, not on the ground, then they become the batter. The second variation involves a wall. Someone stands in front of the wall and throws a ball off the wall in a way that will ricochet into the air towards other kids who are waiting to try to catch it. If you catch it on a fly, then you are up next. The game could also be played as a single person, using the wall to practice catching fly balls. As a child, I often used the side of my house.

9. Box Ball: This game can be adapted for inside or outside use. It involves two or three connected, sidewalk-sized boxes. With two boxes, a small rubber ball is hit back and forth between the boxes on one bounce into the box in front of your opponent, similar to two-square. Failure to hit the ball back properly leads to your opponent getting a point. The winner is determined by who gets the level of points that are agreed upon before play.

The second variation is called **Box Baseball**. Three boxes are used. A person stands at each end of the boxes and pitches a ball into the box in front of the other player. The opponent must hit it back to the box in front of the pitcher while not hitting it into the middle box. If it bounces into the correct box, it is a base hit. The number of times it bounces determines the base total. Innings are played just like baseball. When playing inside, you need a solid surface, like a basement or garage floor. At the office, we played it in the hallways outside my office.

10. Balloon adapted games: In my office, we made simple adaptations of regular, net-style games but using a balloon instead of a ball. Immensely popular was **Balloon Volleyball**. Take two chairs, placed about three feet apart, and place a broom handle across the tops of the chairs to provide a makeshift net. Two or three kids are on either side of the net to play against each other as teams. Scoring can vary from volleyball rules to even tennis rules. Boundaries are designated for automatic outs. I often made up random teams so everyone had a chance to play with other members. Some players even had to wait until they could replace a child in a rotations format. While waiting, they had to cheer for their team and make positive comments to the opposition like, "Nice try!"

Balloon Kickball or Baseball was an adaptation we used inside. Another great game was to play **Keep It Up.** In this game, kids stand or sit in a circle and hit a balloon among themselves. The goal is to see how long they can keep the balloon in the air and not let it touch the floor. A group can be challenged to achieve a certain time limit to earn more points, or before proceeding to another activity. You can also have contests to set records. The office record for Keep It Up was forty-seven minutes. This is a great game to develop teamwork, handle frustrations, and rein in aggressive or impulsive kids.

11. Juggling: Another great group game we made up was team juggling. The group stands in a circle opposite another child. Stuffed animals can be used. An order is developed by having one child start with calling out another child's name and tossing them the stuffed animal. The next child then calls out another and passes the stuffed animal. This continues in the same manner until everyone can keep the same order first developed. Once you can pass it without too much disorder, then a second stuffed animal is introduced into the order. The goal is to keep two objects passing in the same order. Eventually, with my groups, up to four objects could be passed until it all broke down. This is a great activity for developing frustration tolerance and teamwork.

12. Hot Potato: This game is easily adapted for the office. Children sit in a circle and three or four stuffed animals are passed around randomly until someone has two or more in their lap. That child then has to leave the circle and sit at the edge, helping to retrieve stuffed animals that go out of bounds. This continues until two children are left to face each other. This game helps to work on frustration tolerance and sportsmanship.

13. Dodgeball: This game is great for outside or inside activity. Two teams are chosen, and a dodgeball is thrown back and forth. If you are hit and drop the ball, you are out. If you catch a thrown ball, the other player is out. An outside area is created as a playing court. When playing inside, use softer Nerf balls or even stuffed animals, and watch out for breakable objects that may need to be moved out of the way to a safe place. Rules can vary for how many outs are needed to stay in the game — and no "head-hunting."

14. Running Bases: Another outside or inside game. Two bases are set up a certain distance apart. Designate two players to guard the bases while the remaining children try to run between the bases. The guardians try to toss a ball or stuffed animal between them and try to tag the players caught off base. This continues until one child is left and is the winner. Players can vary as to who guards next.

15. Skully: This is one of my favorite games. It adapts well to both inside and outside. When playing outside, use a flat surface like the school yard and, using chalk, create a six-foot square box. Each corner has a corresponding number, either 1, 2, 6, and 8: numbers 5 and 7 are in a box in the center of the board while 3, 4, 9, and 10 are arranged along the edges, opposite from each other. Surrounding the middle is an area designated "lose a turn." Place a "lose a turn" area equally spaced apart in four additional sites.

The playing piece is constructed from bottle caps. To make the caps controllable, melt some crayon wax into the open end. This will give it some weight. Use different crayon colors for each cap. To begin, a player places their cap in the middle and flicks it towards Box 1. You get one flick per turn unless you have landed in the proper numbered box you were aiming at. If it lands in the box, your play can continue to the next number in the order. If you land in "lose a turn," you must skip your next turn. Another player can bump any player into or out of a "lose a turn" space. The object is to get through all the boxes in order, both ascending and descending, and return to the middle where you started. Anywhere from two to six players can play at a time.

Adapting the game for indoor use requires a flat surface. I used the back of my old knock hockey board and played on a smaller scale. The game is set up and played in the same way. One advantage of using the knock hockey board is that the layout of the Skully game can be permanently drawn. This game is great for working on sportsmanship and frustration tolerance.

16. Knock Hockey: This game was great for developing creativity, teamwork, frustration tolerance, and sportsmanship. I often paired up players into teams and used time limits for switching players. While waiting your turn, you must cheer for your partner. If another team scores, you have to say, "Nice shot!" Sometimes I used multiple pucks to press the frustration button.

17. Hula Hoops: There are many ways to make up hoop games aside from the normal use of hip-swinging the hoop. With my younger and impulsive children, hoops became an excellent tool for teaching boundaries and patience. I would place six hoops around the floor in my office with a child standing in each hoop. I would then launch a balloon into the area. Balloons create great random patterns. They could only catch it or hit it if it came into their space. They cannot leave the hoop and interfere with another player. A player must wait patiently for their turn. At times, I used two to three balloons to create unique effects.

Rolling hoops also makes for interesting, inventive games. Try rolling the hoop and see if you can get it to fall around a target.

18. Bowling: Using plastic bottles, soda cans, or milk cartons for pins, a bowling alley can be set up in a driveway or inside of an office space. A large Nerf ball or even a small basketball can be the bowling ball. Scoring is like regular bowling or adjusted creatively. Specialty rolling can be used to make the game more about being silly and fun than about high scores and winning. A silly roll can be to stand backwards at the line and roll it between your legs, or to stand on one leg while rolling it. Players were encouraged to make up other creative, silly rolls.

19. Tag: This is an extremely popular game to play outside. It is also a good lunch time activity at school. Teams are made up or one person is designated "It." The goal is for the "It" or team of "Its" to tag every player on the opposing team while they run around and try to avoid being tagged. A certain boundary should designate the playing area. If you are tagged, you are frozen in place. A frozen player can be saved by another unfrozen player on their team by being tagged. When one team is completely frozen, the game is over. Another variation is to have only one "It" who tries to tag any other player, who then becomes the new "It."

20. Capture the Flag: Two teams are created. An area is designated for the play space. At either end of the area, a flag is placed. It can be any object like a scarf, stuffed animal, etc. The play is between two to four kids. The goal is to run across the area and steal the other team's flag. Players can block passage to the flag.

21. Puppet shows: Puppets can be constructed from socks, paper bags, or even stuffed animals. I had a set of small finger puppets for the office. A table with a tablecloth, blanket, or even coats can be used to make a stage. Children can put on a short show, either by themselves or with a partner.

22. Marbles: This is a finger-shooting game played in a small circle. A target is set up or a set of circles around a bull's eye is constructed. Players shoot their marbles to either get close to the target or push an opponent's marble out of the way. Collecting marbles and trading them was popular among my childhood friends. There are so many different styles of marbles.

23. Flipping sports cards. A sports card has a picture of the player on one side and a history of that player on the other side. This makes for a heads and tails arrangement. A player stands and flips out a preset number of cards. The opposing player must match the cards of the first player. If you cannot match it, then you lose that card. Trading and collecting sports cards was also a major neighborhood activity in my day.

24. Jump rope: In my neighborhood, this was a common game that was a favorite, mostly with the girls. There are many variations involving one or two ropes.

25. Relay races: An obstacle course can be constructed to challenge individuals and teams. How quickly one gets through the course determines the winner. Obstacles can involve leaping, climbing, and crawling. This is a great activity for imagination, teamwork, and fun and can be easily adapted to for playing either outside or inside.

26. Building race cars: In my old neighborhood, summers were often spent building pushcart racers. We would bike to the "dumps," areas where people often discarded old or worn household items such as baby carriages, old crates, and lumber. We would harvest the wheels and add them to the crates to build pushcart racers. We decorated them with old or discarded paint. Teams were made up and races were held. It was important to find streets with hills. Challenges were made between kids on different blocks. We also made small, wooden racers from kits often used by the Boy Scouts. We would carve them, attach wheels, and paint them. A track would be built from scrap wood, and we would hold races.

27. Hide and Seek: An extremely popular game and a great summertime activity, it is also called "Manhunt." It can be played any time but is more effective when played at night. Boundary areas are pre-set; the larger the boundary the better. The general rule is that one team hides while the other seeks them out. Captured players are taken to a holding area but can escape if tagged by another, non-captured teammate. We had many kids on my block, so teams would be large enough to accommodate at least five to ten kids per team. Sometimes we played across many blocks.

Playing indoors requires enough space to provide hiding spots with smaller-sized teams.

Figure 8

MAKE THE BEST OF IT!

Figure 9

It's not

HAT
Horrible, Awful, Terrible

It's only FAD
Frustrating, Annoying, Disappointing

Figure 10
Do you suffer from HAT?

<u>H</u>orrible, <u>A</u>wful, <u>T</u>errible

SAVE THIS

Feel free to take a photo or make a copy of this page, or any of the other signs, and keep them handy for easy reference.

Figure 11

Stay calm and think on your feet

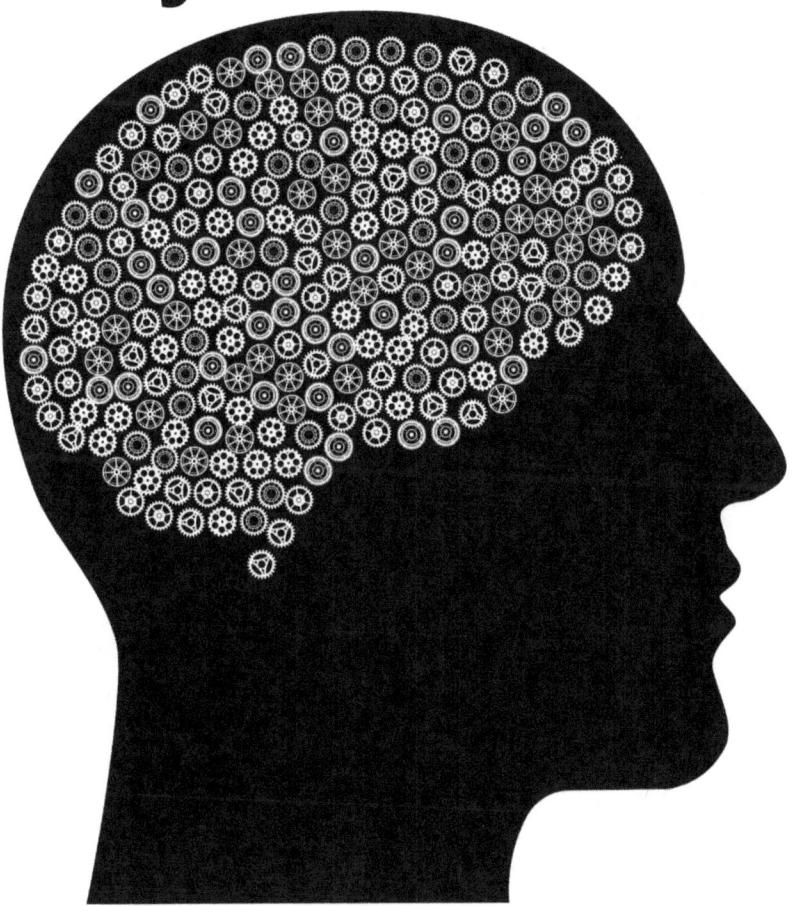

Figure 12

3 STEPS FOR CONFRONTING ANXIETY, FRUSTRATION, ANGER, AND STRESSFUL SITUATIONS

1. Buzz Word
2. Calming or Comforting Image
3. Breathing and Muscle Release

Skill Drill: Handling Teasing

To handle teasing, children must learn how to control their reaction to a teaser. Teasing is a normal part of the growing-up process. We have all gone through it and have survived. Children first use teasing as a way of finding out information about someone else. If a child is too sensitive or overreacts, then other children will find them unpleasant to be with. They can become easy targets for others who will displace their own bad feelings on them. They can also be made fun of for the cruel entertainment of others. If a child is perceived as having low social status, then other children will avoid them for fear of peer rejection.

Children need to learn that no matter how hard they try, there is no absolute method for stopping someone from teasing them. Challenge the child to think of some way they believe they can stop you from calling them a name. Regardless of how creative or persistent they are, there are still alternative ways they can be teased. As an example, even if the child says they can ignore you, tell, or even hit you, show them it is still possible they can be teased. Short of killing you, there is no absolute way they can stop you from teasing them.

Equally important, children must learn that it is what they think about the tease, not the teaser, that makes them upset. Two or more people hearing the same tease can have many different responses. Allow the child to tease you and show them the words have not hurt you. Show them how to think about the tease. For example, if a child calls me a rotten egg, does that automatically turn me into a rotten egg? When they called me names, I would respond loudly saying, "wow," "big deal," "just words," "who cares," "put it on the news," etc. Is it truly horrible, awful, or terrible (HAT)? If someone persists in teasing, all that means is they are someone I might decide not to be friends with.

It is also particularly important that children learn that, no matter how hard they try, it is impossible to absolutely make anyone like us or be our friend.

Someone can offer us lots of money or attention to be friends, yet we can still choose not to like them. All we can do is be friendly which can increase our chances of becoming friends. People often become friends with those who share similar interests. Work at developing your own interests. Friendships based on sharing unique hobbies or interests are often longer lasting.

Ignoring teasers, a popular bit of advice given to children, can at times help to defuse a situation. More often, ignoring may be perceived as a weakness by the peer group and can lead to being teased even more. Becoming aggressive or verbally abusive will only heighten the tension and lead to more aggressive behavior.

I prefer to teach children to make a non-threatening verbal **comeback** response at the time they are teased. A slightly sarcastic comment can help focus the child to keep the tease in perspective. Is it really HAT to be teased? The comeback also sends the message, "I don't care what you said, and I don't need your friendship."

Activities:

The object of this drill is to help the child become desensitized to teasing and make a quick, reflexive, non-threatening verbal comment when teased.

1. Encourage the child to tease you. Demonstrate and model using **comebacks.** These are short, slightly sarcastic comments said boldly and quickly. For example, "gee thanks," "nice comment," "wow, like I really care," "that's nice," "cool," "amazing, put it on the news," "who cares," "tell the President," "God bless you too," etc. Try to emphasize a confident and sarcastic tone. Remember that a comeback is to remind ourselves not to overreact to the tease. It is not meant to stop the teaser. **Comebacks can be any short phrase if it is not nasty or a put down of yourself.**

2. Being comforting and supportive, tell the child that you are now going to tease them. Remind the child to use comebacks. Prompt them to make appropriate comebacks. Be mindful of the tone of voice. Help them to not be wimpy or too aggressive. Be careful not to make the comebacks too silly. Trying to be funny can backfire and make the child look ridiculous. Avoid nasty responses. They can lead to a fight. Being nasty is not the correct value we want to instill in our children.

3. Construct a **comeback list**. Keep a record of a new and favorite comebacks. Update the list regularly. Try to find comebacks that fit their personality.

4. As days and weeks go by and at varying times of the day, sneak attack and tease your child when they do not expect it. Reward them for using a good

comeback. Make corrections and model a more appropriate comeback. Reward them for trying. The object is to make that comeback a reflexive response. This takes many months of practice and periodic review. Reasoning alone will not work.

Skill Drill: Being Positive

Research has demonstrated that having a positive outlook on life is more socially desirable and contributes towards having more friendships. Positive people are more optimistic, happier, accomplish and achieve more, and have better physical health.

Children with impulse problems and social-skill deficits will primarily focus on the negative aspects of a given situation. They also respond negatively. Other children become turned off to a child that whines, complains, tantrums, or is otherwise negative.

A child who focuses on positive aspects will start a chain reaction of positive responses from those around them. Pleasant people are easier to engage and are more enjoyable to be with.

It is well understood that children will model the behavior of others around them. It is particularly important for parents and other adults to be aware of the degree of their own positivity. If you are not a positive person, then working on this drill with your child can most certainly be helpful to your life as well.

Activities:

1. Pick an unusual item and ask the child to find at least 10 positive things to say about it. For example, show a child a crushed can and ask them to find as many positive things as they can about it. For example, you can play a catch or a kick the can game, pretend it is a toy car, it is colorful and be used as a decoration, it can be a paper weight, there is useful information printed on it, it can be recycled, etc. Each day pick another item and practice listing positive comments.

2. Take a rolled-up ball of paper and see how many different games you can make up.

3. When you enter a room or an area, ask the child to focus on what is positive about the space.

4. Practice giving compliments to each other. Say thank you after each compliment.

5. Help the child to make a list of things they enjoy doing. Hang pictures on their bedroom walls that reflect their individual interests. Learn to discover what makes them feel like themselves. Stop worrying about what the "popular" crowd likes to do.

6. Try to teach your child that, in life, there are no failures, only experiences. There is always something to learn from each experience. Success is what we learn from our experiences.

If a child does not perform as well as they expected with an activity, help them to see the outcome is not a failure. Try to get them to see as many positive things as they can from the event. For example, if a child receives a low grade on a test, it is not a failure. Try to state what they learned from the experience, such as improving study skills, getting extra tutorial help, getting more rest or sleep the night before a test, etc. Remember, whatever the outcome, ask, "Was it horrible, awful or terrible?"

Figure 13

Positive Self-Thoughts

Catch yourself worrying

Say Stop!
Take a slow deep breath.

Asks Questions
Where is the evidence that I need to worry now?

How often has what I've been worrying
about has actually happened?
For example: My brother leaving the house or
parents forgetting to pick me up.

Accept ...
...that it will take 10 minutes to clam down
Take off the "HAT."
Catch your breath.

Keep a journal.

Write down what happened.
The Situation:

The negative self-thoughts:

Positive self-thoughts:

Figure 14

Be a Positive Person

Figure 15

Figure 16

IF YOU HAD FUN, THEN YOU WON!

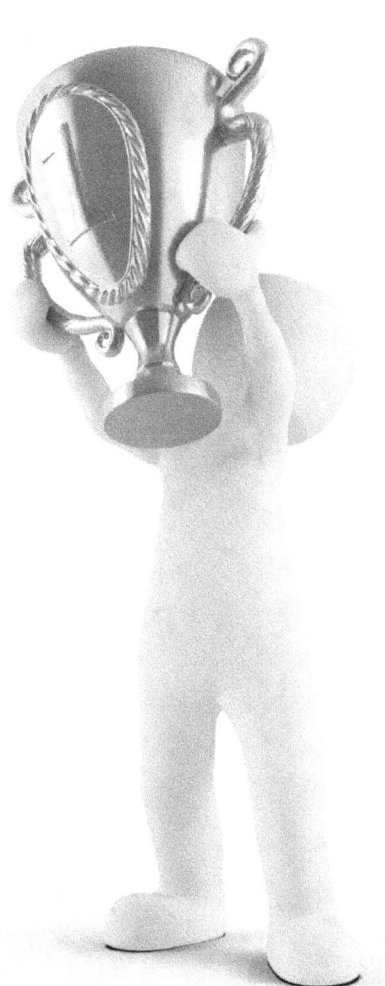

Figure 17
There Are No Failures!

There Are Only Experiences You Can Learn From!

As You Learn You Succeed!

Skill Drill: Why Did You Do That?

The object of this drill is to help children who are either impulsive or passive learn to respond appropriately when someone intrudes into their space. Children with attention-deficit/hyperactivity disorder, oppositional defiant disorder, a learning disability, or anxiety disorder miss social cues and can either respond impulsively or passively to events around them. The impulsive child makes a quick, out-of-control decision to rush forward verbally and/or physically, exacerbating and prolonging the situation. The passive child will often under-respond and become a victim of aggression by others. Their responses are often made without malicious intent. They lack the natural ability to momentarily hold back responding in order to survey the situation and find a more suitable response.

The impulsive child often develops a different worldview from children with an easier-to-control neurological system. These children do not connect the dots of life very well. Do you recall sequencing pictures that required to connect the dots in a continuous, numerical order? If you follow it correctly, you get a nice picture. Children with impulsivity lose the order and wind up with a disaster. The passive child becomes overwhelmed and gives up.

To follow a sequence of events to reach a meaningful positive outcome requires the ability to control the flow of information. Withdrawing or rushing forward without considering all the factors brings about a spiral of negative responses that leads to more frustration for the child. Social rejection, labeling, and disciplinary problems are more frequent for these children. For example, a child with impulsivity sitting at their desk that is bumped by a passing child or teased by another student may quickly respond by pushing, shoving, and making inappropriate comments. The passive child falls and starts to apologize or blame themselves for being in the way. If teased, they may cry. As this happens, a teacher now pays attention to the commotion. The teaser sits down and acts innocent. The overreacting, impulsive child is whisked off to the office for disciplinary action. The passive child is laughed at. Parents tell their children to avoid these children and a reputation is borne.

The goal of this drill is to teach these children to make a verbal comment that would allow them time to find an appropriate response and avoid over-responding or passively withdrawing. If they can make a better response, they can stop the negative spiral from developing.

The response I liked to teach these children was to ask the question, **"Why did you do that?"**

By asking a question, the child starts to collect information which increases the number of options available to help them choose a better response for the situation. The child who was bumped can ask, **"Why did you do that?"** The other child may say, "I am sorry, it was an accident." This may solve the problem easily. If the response from the teaser is, "I don't like you," the impulsive or passive child can use a **comeback** and tell the other child, "I don't like you either." The impulsive or passive child can also calmly seek an adult to discuss this. Asking, **"Why did you do that?"** in a firm, non-threatening voice can also attract the attention of an adult who can quickly see who really was responsible for the problem.

It is not a typical response for impulsive or passive children to ask a question, such as, **"Why did you do that?"** To acquire this skill, considerable practice, roleplaying, and modeling is required.

I made learning this response a vital skill to teach in all my social-skill groups from my five-year-olds through high schoolers. The skill should be practiced every week. With young children, it is difficult to have a logical discussion about this technique. Older children can engage in a discussion of the merit of asking questions. As they acquire the desired response, I will, without warning, periodically bump them, take a toy away, or knock something of theirs over. They earn credit by making the correct **"Why did you do that?"** response.

Parents should practice the skill at home. Take 15 minutes each day and practice the response. Remind your child it is time to practice. At this stage of training, make sure the session is not scheduled when a child is actively involved in another activity, such as a play date. Plan the session when you are prepared to play with the child. As you play, take an object from them or bump into the child. Remind them to ask, **"Why did you do that?"** If the child responds correctly, give them verbal praise or a small treat or token. Encourage the child to do that to you and model the **"Why did you do that?"** response. Do this daily for two weeks.

After two weeks, try using the response at other times around the house while other activities are ongoing. Outside of the home, try practicing first in mildly distracting places, then gradually practice as the situations are more involved or distracting. Remind the child you will be practicing the **"Why did you do that?"** response. Reward the child for correct responses, or model the correct response if they make a mistake. In later weeks, periodically sneak attack the child and reward or correct their responses. The goal is to teach the question response to become an automatic reaction.

As you practice, vary your responses to the **"Why did you do that?"** question. At times say, "I am sorry, it was an accident," while at other times say, "I don't like you," or, "I don't want to be your friend." Encourage the use of comebacks, like "big deal" or "who cares." Children need cueing and prompting. Be patient. Impulsive children can often forget to be patient.

Figure 18

Figure 19

WORRYING DOES NOT TAKE AWAY TOMORROW'S TROUBLES.

IT TAKES AWAY TODAY'S PEACE.

SAVE THIS

Feel free to take a photo or make a copy of this page, or any of the other signs, and keep them handy for easy reference.

Figure 20

To overcome your fears:

1. Stop and catch your breath!

2. Think of something good!

3. Set small goals or steps!

Social Skills Groups

Pros and Cons:
Pros: Real life experiences, immediate feedback, quick reinforcement, club like camaraderie, better chance for generalizing behavior.
Cons: Control and management issues increase such as; fit between group members ages and level of disability, increased planning, more phone contacts and parent meetings,coordinating schedules, increased paper work and record keeping, availability of space and flow of incoming new group members, comfort level of working with more than one patient at a time.

Main Objectives:
Ages 5-7:
1. Adjust to token economy.
2. Develop awareness of boundaries; stay in place at circle time and group play with or without hula hoops. Recognize stop signs.
3. Increase eye contact. Raising your hand before speaking and finding my eye contact. Look at others when speaking.
4. Taking turns and sharing. Play simple balloon games and passing games.
5. Being positive drills: giving a nice greeting and compliment; identify positive qualities by using what's positive drill.
6. How to tell a simple joke?
7. Share a simple event such as favorite shows or toy, etc.
8. Memory and listening skills: recall what someone said; recall what you saw about a person, start stop drills using games like musical chairs and Simon Says.

Socialized Child
Figure 21

Self
Biological needs
Developmental stage
Innate personality traits
Verbal/Language ability
Intelligence
Self Interests - What makes you feel like you?

Home
Home style
Parental model
Home school respect - living
Parents' role with self esteem

School
Teacher's Lesson Plan
  1. Socialization lessons
  2. Teamwork
  3. Curiosity
  4. Accept Individual differences
    with rules and responsibilities
Group play in class
Structured recess time

Therapy
Social skill training
Anger/frustration control
Excessive thinking - how to think
Read your body
Coordination of home & school

Figure 22

Planning a Social Event Worksheet

1. Biology Remember to consider age, type of disability, health, hunger/ nutrition, fatigue and medication requirements with side affects, etc:

_____
_____
_____
_____
_____
_____

2. Environmental
  b) Activities characteristics such as interest level, organization and sensory over load:
  c) Your personal issues such as disposition, emotional needs, age, fatigue and stress level:
  d) Identify roles and responsibilities for parents:

_____
_____
_____
_____
_____

3. Preparations
  a) Define the tasks to be learned. Break into small steps:
  b) Role play and model:
  c) Materials you will need to bring along:

_____
_____
_____
_____

9. Verbal defense drills: how to handle teasing using comebacks, hot seat drill, assertion skill of why did you do that?

10 Creative play, create a game, being silly; if you had fun you won.

11. Being a good leader. Pretend that your friends are at your home. A) Pick a game or activity for all of us to play. B) Don't grab rule. C) Your friends pick and go first. D) Set rules such as how many items can be taken. E) Make decisions and settle conflicts: do over and rock paper scissors

12. How to be a good participant. Ask the leader, share toys, asking someone to join, be a good partner.

13. Sportsmanship skills such as cheering, encourage by saying good try, not bragging, no cheating. Handle losing, survivor drills and finding how to help out while you wait.

14. Clean up and work together

15 Take a calm out when upset. Go to safety zone and move away to calm down.

Ages 8-10:

Additional skill drills include all of the earlier age drills and objectives, but also include additional skills.

1. Greater emphasis on anger/frustration management skills: Stop, Step Back, Breathe and Think. Learn that feelings come from how you think about events. It's Not HAT! Develop problem-solving skills. Make The Best Of It!

2. How to reinforce others for positive behavior. Use token economy to encourage members to give points to others. Look for the good in others to find the good in you.

3. Group discussions about events that are troubling someone. Develop empathy skills.

4. Greater emphasis on complex conversations skill: 1:1, meeting new people, small group, lunch table talk, and breaking in.

Ages 11-13:

Additional skill drills include all of the earlier age drills, but also include more emphasis on the following additional skills.

1. Making group decisions. How to respect those whose opinions were rejected and be fair.

2. Judging your own behavior. Determine your own point score.

3. Self-expression: create more complex games, silly acting, and role-plays, being noticed for your positive traits.

4. Working in more complex teamwork events such as the office Olympics.

5. Social awareness: what's current with kids, being aware of changes in style, language and biological changes.

Ages 13-15:
Additional skill drills include all of the earlier age drills, but group dynamics takes on a greater emphasis.

1. At this stage I shift to a more experiential basis. These kids often reject classroom-type of lessons. There are lessons for handling teasing, conversation skills, and anger/frustration skills. More time is set apart for talking about our lives to bring out issues for discussion. More talk on sexuality and the changing social world, i.e., drugs, dating, family issues, hot social topics.

2. Where do I fit in? Develop your own distinctive interests and style. Finding your own kind in social, school and community activities. Accepting other styles without feeling inferior.

3. Encouraged to hang out with each other and visit each other.

Managing Children with Attention-deficit Hyperactivity Disorder

By Michael Simon, Ph.D.

Workshop: Managing Behavior

Often the failure of behavior modification to bring about change is due to many factors. Some of the problems relate to the inability to find an appropriate reward or reinforcer, lack of knowledge in behavioral technology, and the specific problems of the patient. Many times, I have been called upon by anxious parents to perform "behavior modification" to eliminate ADHD. Often, my first task was to explain that there is no miracle "behavior modification" that will stop or cure ADHD.

When treating ADHD, the first place to begin is with learning how to manage this condition. It is a lifelong task. Helping people to succeed begins with learning to modify the environment to minimize frustration and failure. Secondly, teach, through life experiences, a strategy for how to organize and control their world. Initially it is the job of caretakers, such as parents. Later the person will need to know how to arrange his or her own personal environment to maximize success.

In my view, the treatment of ADHD is learning how to manage the flow of information in a person's life. Often the issue is a figure/ground problem. People with ADHD often focus first on the non-essential details of a situation and either under- or over-respond to the wrong information or details around them. One of the main problems associated with ADHD is that it affects the ability to make proper choices and then to plan a suitable response to a situation to maximize a favorable outcome. It is this mindset that requires modification. If one can't see the reinforcer, or is unable to understand or commit to what the proper response should be, then one cannot succeed.

The treatment of ADHD relies upon managing both the biological and environmental factors in a person's life. If these factors are the main focus of intervention, then a person can grow to learn how to manage their life.

Exercise #1: Imagine that you are a parent with a handicapping condition such as blindness, deafness, or physical impairment. What changes would you make in yourself to increase your ability to help your child?

Exercise #2: If your child were physically disabled, such as wheelchair-bound, what changes would you make in the child's environment to help that child succeed?

With ADHD, parents often do not realize that this is an issue that is biological. It is often easier for parents to accept having to make changes within themselves and/or the environment of the child when they can see an obvious physical deficit, such as an impaired limb.

The Early Years: Birth to Age 6

It Begins With Biology:

The young child is mostly controlled by biological factors, such as hunger, fatigue, temperature, illness, sound, allergies, sensory overload, sensory deficits, biological drive, energy level, and impaired brain functioning. Time spans are minutes long. They respond to what is immediately happening. These factors often will dictate, whether a parent likes it or not, what the child will do.

Children are not born blank. They come into the world with so many biologically-determined issues that control their behavior. In addition, children inherit their biological personality. They will resemble their parents' family traits. Shyness, quick temper, disorganization, and moodiness are often inborn traits. A parent who also has ADHD needs to remember how they learned to cope with their biological nature. Parents can also be helped to relate to their child's frustration if they can remember how they felt as their parents struggled to handle their ADHD problems.

Knowing your child's biological limitations can affect how you arrange going about your daily lives. When a child's biological limits are strained, they often resort to very primitive methods of communicating their displeasure, such as crying, withdrawing, rushing forward out of control, and temper tantrums. A child with ADHD who gets overwhelmed may become shy and withdrawn just to reduce the flow of sensory information. A child with ADHD may be unable to gain control of sensory information and become overly aggressive, get a sudden burst of energy, and rush forward into a danger zone.

To handle these biological problems, parents have to plan around these issues. Remember, the goal is to help the child control the flow of information coming into their brain. To control these biological factors, parents need to arrange the environment of the child or alter the biological functioning of the child's body.

Environmental Arrangements:

Daily schedules need to be considered. A parent must adjust to the child's level of development. It is difficult to expect the child to adjust easily to a world that is very busy, revolving around the needs of the parent. Pressing a child beyond their limits will result in a very upset child and stressed out parent. As the parent stresses out, often it is the child that is blamed, hit, yelled at, and feels like a failure. When your expectations, schedule, and lifestyle are adjusted to reflect the child's limitations, then the child receives better attention and grows up feeling more loved.

Common problem areas often revolve around the scheduling of routines, such as parent work schedules, shopping, meal times, sleep patterns, playtime activities, education programs, and teaching hygiene, dressing, and table manners. In fact, in all areas of a child's life, there needs to be special adjustments made in order for the child to gain control over the flow of information to hopefully increase the chances that the child can make proper responses. A child who can't handle the flow of information often receives increased negative consequences. People with ADHD often can't transition from activity to activity easily. Planning for changing activities needs to be taken into consideration when shifting schedules.

Biological Arrangements:

ADHD is a biological problem. When the environment can't be adjusted enough because the child's biology is so much a factor, then parents might have to try to adjust the child's internal biological reactions.

Medications are often required to help adjust the flow of information in and out of the brain. One can't succeed if the body can't allow for the proper response to be made. For example, if you need glasses, try spending a few days going about your life without them. Please be very careful if you try this experiment! A child who can't pick up the sensory information can't make the required response. It would be unfair to punish the child because their brain won't allow for the proper response. Rewards will be unable to be earned if the brain can't control the body. Remember, if someone require glasses, you can't reward them to see better without glasses.

Diet and Allergy problems can affect how a child biologically functions. Some people with ADHD are very reactive to certain food groups as well as vitamin and nutrient levels in their bodies. Attention needs to be given to watch for patterns of behavior changes following the ingestion of certain food groups. The essential food and/or allergy condition that can negatively affect a person will vary for each person. It is not true for all children that sugars will make ADHD worse.

Sensory Integration and Auditory Processing problems, again, will affect the ability of a child with ADHD to correctly identify the proper message and/or make the proper response. The child does not deliberately want to make the wrong behavior, but is responding to the information they have perceived.

If the perception is impaired, then the behavior will be out of context with the current situation.

Messages should be simple and clear. Time-frame expectations should be adjusted as the child ages. Time-frame expectations will usually have to be shorter for this condition. Timers can help young children measure time while waiting. Memory functions can also be quite a problem with ADHD. Verbal instructions often don't make it to short-term memory, and forgetfulness is a common sensory/brain problem.

Exercise can also be an important part of helping a child with ADHD. Many of these children require a period of active, daily exercise. With many people, exercise helps to activate neurological functioning.

Security Factors will affect both Biological and Environmental Arrangements:

These factors relate to the emotional world of the family. Parents' problems with their lives will greatly affect their ability to handle the difficult world of an ADHD child. If, as an adult, your life is out of control, then your child's life, ADHD or not, will be out of control. Yelling, hitting, screaming, crying, lecturing, or begging your child to behave will not work. Parents who resort to these approaches will only excite the child more. Extreme negative emotional behavior by the parents only models more inappropriate behavior for the child. A child with sensory/perception problems will only become more confused. In later years, they will use your negative emotional responses against you to manipulate you into giving them their way, or as an excuse for inappropriate behavior.

Parents need to work as a team. Each parent has a day job, be it at home or at a place of business, as well as a second job on the night shift at home. At times, one or both of you may burn out. As good partners, one of you will have to hold down the fort while the other gets to engage in an activity to clear their mind and soul. The raising of children necessitates that parents **grow up** and accept new responsibilities. Parents need to agree on strategies for how to raise children. If you contradict each other, then agree to disagree and seek information.

Staying in love means accepting change and adjusting your life to where you are now in your lives, rather than demanding that life return to those easier days when you first fell in love. Single parents will have a harder time but still need to find someone to help give them a hand. ADHD does not stop with divorce.

Your personal habits will often affect how well your child functions. You must learn to **manage your own behavior**. How you react to frustration, annoyance, and disappointment will be greatly challenged by any child. Personal problems with your health, level of rest and exercise, moodiness, and social outlets can overwhelm you and need to be addressed. If you are emotionally overwhelmed, it will be very difficult to keep to schedules, keep your home orderly, and have patience to solve problems.

ADHD children require a home life that has routines, an environment that is tidy, addresses rest, diet and exercise, is calm, loving, playful, and reflective of the age of the child. If, as in many situations, the parent has an ADHD condition, then the parent needs treatment as well. The main issues for the young child revolve around how well **Biology and Security** are handled. Thinking and reasoning are not well-developed brain processes in the young child.

Social needs are not that prominent. Very young children do not require or need a ton of play-dates and friendships. Social activities should be highly structured, short in duration, and limited to the biological development of the particular child. The parent of a child with ADHD will have to be very active in coordinating play and may have to join the child when interacting with other children. Again, the focus should be on the management of the flow of information into a child's brain and the ability to make a correct response. For example, a parent may find himself or herself in the sandbox at the playground helping their child play with other children, particularly if the child can't easily process the movement of other children who are also in the sandbox. It may not be a time for socializing with the other parents. The child who is unable to handle the sandbox and/or other playground activity may soon develop a bad reputation and will be shunned by other children and parents.

The Middle Years: Six to Twelve Years Old

At this stage of development, the child can now often begin and develop the ability to delay gratification, become aware of greater time frames, understand cause and effect, and live in a **rule**-based household. The child now begins to reflect a growing sense of **self** and **social** involvement. They will express more opinions and start planning how to control or manipulate their parents, friends, teachers, and social world. Parents can no longer expect to have the last word, but they can have the last privilege! It is a time to expect children to do more for themselves. We should expect them to take on more responsibilities with **Home, School and Respect.**

Home:

At this point, we want children to learn to start cleaning up their rooms, pick up mess they leave inside and outside the house, do some chores, and maintain hygiene. Rewards and punishments won't work alone for children with ADHD. Parents still need to be mindful of the need to **organize the flow of information** so the child can make a **choice** whether they will follow the rule and earn the reward, or face the consequences of not having what they want. For example, sending a child with ADHD to clean up their room, without addressing the organization of information factor, will often result in the child becoming lost among the mess. **Managing** the amount of mess and being able to focus on what needs to be done will more often determine if they earn the reward, no matter which reward it is.

Your complete home needs to be kept **organized**, which includes the parents' living space as well. Don't let your home turn into a toy store or city dump. Develop a toy closet or area where the flow of toys can be controlled. Weed out old broken toys, rotate certain toys according to the season, and have toy bins that are easily accessible. Have a laundry hamper in the child's room.

I expect a child with ADHD to be able to clean their room. A clean room means picking up toys, putting laundry away, picking up papers and tissues, and straightening out the bed. This should be done daily. Give the child a **clipboard** with a **list** of what has to be done. The list becomes a tool to help the child remember and focus on what needs to be done. Teach your child a path to follow when it is time to clean. With younger children, parents will need to spend time teaching good clean-up habits. **Keep consistent** clean-up routines and schedules. The rewarding activity should follow the work that needs to be done. If they have a list, then they can stay more focused and succeed. Verbal instructions without any **visual** aids are less effective. Remember, the goal is to increase **sensory** reception.

Chores are also handled with lists, consistency, and patience. Routines and schedules will be helpful. Each child needs some chores. Doing chores helps build **character**. Children need to learn how to give back to the family and not just grow up taking from the family. A child with ADHD needs to have visual tools so they can stay on task and learn to be responsible. If you send them on an errand in the house, give them a **Post-it note**. This may help them visually remember.

Auditory commands can be easily forgotten due to sensory deficits. Remember, the further away you are from the child when giving a verbal command, the more difficult it will be for them to hear you against the surrounding background sounds of the environment. A parent often has to be about an arms' distance away from a child to get their attention. Eye contact is also very important. Having the child repeat the command may help to increase memory.

The house should be put back together by the end of the night. Allowing things to get way out of control will only overwhelm the child and make it harder for them to control the sensory information flow. Schedule clean-up periods around common family events, for example, put some things away before sitting down for dinner, before evening TV time, or before nighttime rituals, such as the bedtime story. Waking up to an uncluttered home can make your mornings easier. Having family clean-up times is a good way to get everyone involved.

Try not to schedule too many after school extra-curricular events, such as sports, religion, and clubs. Too many of these events in a week will overwhelm the child's sensory system. Extra events will add unnecessary stress which will result in increased frustration and failure. Some children can benefit from having down time. If possible, having a basement or rumpus room can be a good place for some of these kids to be allowed to expend energy. Keep that room child-friendly. They will jump around.

School:

It is important to have a good working relationship with your child's teacher. Your child's teacher should have an understanding of your child's ADHD learning style. Often adjustments need to be made with the class-work in order to keep the child on task and motivated. Smaller amounts of work with more frequent reinforcement may help the child stay focused. Biological treatments may still have to be used in school if attention span and motor activity interfere with learning.

A **checklist** may help a child to remember what they have to bring home from school and what to take back to school. Teachers should direct the child to their checklists so the child can learn to monitor their own behavior and become less dependent. Checklists can be laminated and attached to the backpack where they will be visible. A feedback or assignment-pad system needs to be used to record essential information. Some children can benefit by using a **tape recorder** to keep track of information when visual distractibility is an issue.

The **backpack** needs to be opened and cleaned out daily. **Color code** the files where homework is placed. Use a red folder, for example, for math homework and other colors for other subjects. When an assignment is finished, place a red dot on the top of the page and place it in the red folder. Use other color dots for other folders. This will help the child organize and retrieve material. Each day, look at the assignment pad or listen to the tape and transfer information onto a master **calendar** that is placed over the child's desk or work area at home. Tests are marked with red ink, reports with green ink, and special days, such as gym class, with another color.

Homework is done with respect to the child's biological needs. Some children need a time to rest and exercise after school. Other children need to get down to work right after school because they are losing attention span due to medication limits and fatigue. Help the child draw up a plan for the workload. **Prioritize** the degree of difficulty of the assignments, and plan the work accordingly. Break longer assignments into smaller units. Use templates to block out distractions on the page. Covering up the other problems on a page can help the child stay focused on a task.

For longer assignments, use a board game to increase motivation. For example, after a few math problems or spelling sentences, let the child take a turn on the game. Having fun while working can keep a child working on tasks that the child finds unpleasant.

Use a **tape recorder** to record what a child wants to remember when they have written work, such as a report. Often the task of writing can distract a child and make them forget what they wanted to say. Playing back a tape recording can refresh their memory. When reading for a book report, have the child record information on a tape recorder as they read along so they can retrieve it later when it is time to prepare the report.

The homework and study area needs to be free of distractions. Some children need to hear steady, soft music or **background** sound tapes, such as ocean sounds, to keep them from auditory distractions in the house. They will need frequent checking to be encouraged to keep working.

Studying for a test may require many days of advanced study to get information into long-term **memory**. Reward the effort a child makes, not the test score! Should the child have a problem with a task, work on a plan to correct the problem. A child may need special instruction on study skills or extra tutoring to get the point.

Teaching **problem-solving** skills can help sharpen a child's awareness of alternative responses. Often children with ADHD rush to commit to the first possible response they see and fail to notice other, better alternatives. Game playing can be used to build up the mindset to step back and look at all possibilities before making a game move.

Respect:

Discipline should follow a **positive** model of rewarding efforts. Focusing on the take-aways and threats distracts the child with fear. If you're yelling, then most likely you are not handling stress well! If a child is using their tools and trying to make a good effort, then they should earn their privileges. If a child is having anger-management problems, then they may need instruction on anger-management skills. Anger-management training involves teaching a child to stop, step back to a safe place to discharge their emotions, engage in breathing control, and then rethink the situation. Children should learn to take a **Calm Out** to get refocused.

Disrespectful behavior modeled by the parents will result in the child learning to be disrespectful. Manners, politeness, and respect are learned best when parents demonstrate these qualities.

Many children with ADHD often misread social cues. When this happens, they may need social-skill training programs to teach social skills. Again, the understanding is that ADHD is a biological problem that interferes with the acquisition of information and the determination of a response. When problems occur, the focus should be toward teaching the child a new behavior and not condemning the child's inappropriate behavior.

The biological and security issues that dominated the child's early life will continue to present problems that will need to be addressed in this next stage. The child in this middle stage will still require that management modifications be continued while they learn to deal with new expectations regarding managing Home, School, and Respect issues. If these earlier needs are still out of control, then the child will continue to fail and eventually develop emotional problems. Behavior-modification technology will not work if the child's world is not managed well. Parents and children need to learn how to manage themselves and their environment. If you work well in the early and middle years, then life in the next stage, teen years, will be less stressful.

The Management of
Adult Attention-deficit/Hyperactivity Disorder:
Uncluttering Your Home and Workplace

By Michael Simon, Ph.D. March 2006

Attention-deficit/hyperactivity disorder (ADHD), is a condition defined by impulsive, distracted, and, at times, hyperactive behavior. There are many factors that can cause ADHD. They vary from genetic conditions, neurological disorders, diet and nutritional deficiencies, to other bio-chemical imbalances.

ADHD is an information-processing disorder. It is the brain's inability to perceive relevant information, stay on task, and factor out irrelevant, distracting details that results in inappropriate responding. My cognitive and behavioral approach to treatment is to find ways to enhance the brain's ability to focus on essential details that would trigger the proper set of expected behavior. Other disciplines can treat information-processing problems that can interfere with sensory input, such as needing to wear glasses or having a disease, by using medical and other biological methods. These can be essential considerations. It is still important to learn to identify the **trigger**, follow a **plan**, stay on **task,** and **evaluate** the outcome.

The following examples will help to demonstrate these principles.

1. Consider toileting behavior. Early in life our parents taught us to recognize a biological trigger. Remember the pee-pee or I-gotta-go dance? The awareness of that certain feeling tells us which elimination function needs attention. With consistent attention to that **trigger**, we learned to follow a **plan** or series of tasks to relieve ourselves. We learned to stay on **task** until we fulfilled our need, then **evaluated** our performance as successful and experienced a positive sense of relief. Some of us even incorporated the next triggered behavior of washing our hands. Alas, for some members of society, lowering the toilet seat was not easily incorporated due to the non-essential need for males to sit to urinate. Sitting was not necessary for staying on task. Without a trigger signal, learning is inconsistent.

2. When driving a car, a red or green traffic light is an extraordinarily strong trigger for a series of essential responses. The color of the light initiates different action plans. Staying on task is easy to observe and the successful outcome is easy to evaluate. As we learn to drive, the attention to a **trigger** color is a highly visible signal, initiating a **plan** for how we will control the vehicle. The **task** is easy to repeat consistently, and immediate reinforcement is noted by the **evaluation** of successfully controlling the car.

If the traffic light signal is missed, the result cannot be understated. A red traffic light resonates highly in our minds as a danger signal. It is very predictable. Miss the trigger, do not stop, and something horrible will most likely to occur. That is why the driver should be shielded from distractions such as cell phones, noisy kids, conversations with passengers, sleep deprivation, and driving while under the influence.

The goal is to teach an individual to set up easy-to-spot triggers, have them practice attending to that trigger, follow a set pattern of steps, and evaluate the success of their actions. People with ADHD often fail to find the trigger, practice the new habit, and make a positive evaluation. Most often they rush into a situation, pick up a non-essential trigger point, follow a haphazard plan, and make a poor evaluation of themselves. They conclude they cannot do anything correctly, get emotional, and become self-defeating.

Many people with ADHD forget to notice the thousands of triggers they follow correctly in other activities of daily living or their job, like using a phone, using the remote control device to activate the TV, making change, and general social conversation. The list is endless. Where deficiencies are found, the task is to set a new **trigger** in place, develop a simple **plan**, practice the **tasks**, **evaluate** the outcome, then see what you learn and adjust.

Positive Mental Attitude

Having a positive mental attitude is so important when you begin taking control over you behavior. The task of change is exceedingly difficult, even worse if you beat yourself up when you get frustrated. There is a choice: you can either live on the Failure Road of life or live on the Experience Road of life.

Failure Road: On this road of life, when things are not going well, one rushes to conclude that the event is a catastrophe. "Oh my god! This is **H**orrible, **A**wful, and **T**errible!" (HAT). We act irrationally with anger, get defensive with our self-esteem and attack, or put ourselves down and avoid or withdraw into depression. On this path, we accomplish less and are unhappier with life.

HAT events are actually those that are life threatening, like wars, earthquakes, tsunamis, hurricanes, etc. Most events in our daily lives are far from that level! When we take non-HAT events to that level, intense biological reactions occur that distract us from productive problem solving. It is important to learn to take the HAT off!

The Experience Road: On this road, when things are not going according to plan, we step back, take a good deep breath, and think, "I may not like what has happened, but it's not HAT. I wish it could have gone better, but it's only **F**rustrating, **A**nnoying, and **D**isappointing," (FAD). Normally the word "fad" means a short-term event or trendy item that will lose its importance as time passes. The same can be said about FAD events. It may rain today, but the sun will come out tomorrow, bet your bottom dollar.

On the Experience Road, the focus is on what we can learn from every situation. It is accepted that we are always learning throughout our entire lives.

By learning, we are succeeding. There are no failures, only events we can learn from. On this road, it is never an issue of self-esteem. It is accepted that we are born wonderful, free of any emotional issues. No one can take that away from us.

On the Road to Uncluttering

Be mindful of your mindset. Rome was not built in a day. Take small steps. Work on a few new triggers at a time. Reserve time daily to go over your plan. Try to keep your family and friends input to a minimum. Too many cooks spoil the brew! If your home is a disaster, then be willing to accept the assistance of a calm friend or significant other to enforce throwing away unneeded junk.

Watching home and garden TV shows can be a good source of helpful information and organizational tips. Home organization companies are also available for such tasks as closet-building. There are also services where someone can come to your home and set up organization. With this, there is concern of cost and problems of dependency, or regression if you do not change your habits.

Keep in mind these helpful mottos:

1. "Rarely" does not exist. If you have used an item less than one or two times over the course of years, then throw it out. For example, that old chair you are holding onto that you have been planning to fix up when you find the time? Yeah, right.

2. Phone calls can wait. When you are working on a task, keep distractions away. The phone will eat up a lot of time that should be directed towards your new steps.

3. File the "sometimes," throw out the "rarely." In filing, it will be necessary to put away items you need access to "sometimes" but not "daily," such as paid bills, insurance, and other important papers. Non-essential "rarely" items, like junk mail, should go directly into the trash can.

4. Work hard now, feel better later. Immediate pleasure is not the goal. It will be tough at first. Stay on the Experience Road, and take pleasure in what you are learning from your actions.

5. Hey, I am doing a Martha Stewart. Have a role model to look up to. What would Martha do in this situation? Remember, keep it legal.

6. When in doubt, make a list. Write it down. Do not keep ideas and plans in your head. Lists make excellent triggers for action plans.

The Two Roads of Life

Figure 23

ROOM: _____

Things that BELONG	Things that DON'T BELONG

Uncluttering Your Home

1. Clear your mind. Breathe deeply, and take a few moments to get calm and ready to work. Pace yourself — no need to rush. Keep a **notepad** ready to jot down things to remember so your mind can stay clear.

2. Buy a file cabinet. Making files is essential for collating and retrieving information. Each file should be for one type of information, such as paid phone bills, mortgage statements, checks, insurance policies, birth certificates, etc. Keep your files in alphabetical order.

3. Get three boxes. One should be bigger than the other two. In the largest box will go items to be immediately thrown away. Remember, "rarely" does not exist. The next box will be for items that need to be filed for "sometimes" use, either in the file cabinet or storage closet. The last box will be for needed "daily" items, such as notes for school, laundry tickets, bills to be paid, etc.

4. Pick a room to start. Do not take the worst first. Let's gain some confidence. Stand by the entry point. Make **two lists.** One list has what belongs in this room, while the other is a list of what does not belong. Using the kitchen for example, what belongs are dishes, appliances, some furniture, utensils, cleaning solvents, table needs like napkins, food and storage containers, garbage disposal items, certain decorations like flowerpots, things that hang on the fridge, etc. Things that do not belong may be shoes, a tennis racket, jackets, junk mail, old newspaper piles, overflowing garbage cans, schoolwork, etc. You could use a chart like the one below to help.

Keep a special container for daily mail. Important reminder notes can hang on a fridge or be listed on a notepad, or even on a family calendar attached to the fridge.

5. Learn a search pattern. Do not rush headstrong into the center of the room. Start at the doorway. Hold your list of what does not belong. This list and standing at the door are your trigger. Place your arms shoulder-width apart out in front of you. This encompasses your search area. Moving in a circle with your arms out, take two steps forward, stop, look within the outstretched arms, and ask yourself if you see anything on your "does not belong" list. If so, figure out which of the three boxes to place it in. Keep repeating the steps until you are back to the entry point.

Establish the **same search habit** each time you do a room check. As you stand at the entryway, stop to evaluate. Be positive. Even if it seems awkward at first, the search will become faster and easier as time goes on. Return items to proper places. "Daily" stuff, such as clothing, is put where it belongs, like in a closet or given to the person it belongs to. The "sometimes" stuff goes into a file or placed in a closet for items like brooms, magazine racks, etc. Throw away the "rarely" stuff such as junk mail, old newspapers, etc.

Go back to your starting point and take your list, hold out your arms, and repeat the search path. Pick up and sort anything you have now found.

Now that the clutter is away, it will be easier to do the basic cleaning, such as wiping down tabletops, sweeping, and mopping. Make a list of these basic tasks and check off when they are completed.

6. Get a large calendar and affix it to your fridge. Using a different color marker to represent each different room, indicate on what day and time you will unclutter that room. It could be daily or less often, depending on the room. Throughout each day, take several moments to **look** at the calendar. This is your first trigger. On the day or time to do the cleanup, take out your lists and do the search circuit. So, for example, the den might be a red capital D and placed on Monday, Thursday, and Saturday at noon. That means you will do an uncluttering on those days around that time for that room.

7. Establish a central message center. Select a spot on the fridge next to the calendar. Place a notepad divided into two columns. One half is titled the **Do List,** the other is the **Call List.** As events occur during the week, write them down on the correct list. Try to look at the lists frequently during the day. Set a trigger to look at the lists when you finish a meal. Get used to saying to yourself or family, "Check the list." Only keep the calendar and notepad on the fridge. Do not place other items, such as good test grades, decorations, or coupons on the fridge. Too many items will keep you from noticing the trigger list and calendar.

Uncluttering Your Workplace

As you tackle your workplace, keep in mind all that you have learned to this point. Set triggers, plan, stay on task, and evaluate the outcome. Stay on the Experience Road.

1. Your desk or work setting is your base. If you have a desk, then **file cabinets** will be essential. Make a **file** for each new category of information. Each day, only take out the files you are working with. The rest need to stay in the file cabinet or drawer.

2. Keep a **desk calendar** that shows one week at a time and is also divided into hourly intervals. Use color highlighters to mark important dates. Colors help triggers to stand out.

3. Take a notepad. Divide it in half. On one side will be your **Call List,** the other side is the **Do List**. Begin each day checking and updating your lists. During the day, add new items and cross out completed items. At the end of the day, rewrite your lists so they are ready for the next day. Prioritize your lists. Highlight events or calls that must be made.

4. Keep a **clock** on your desk. Time can be an especially important trigger.

5. Keep a small container for pens, pencils, and clips on your desk.

6. Set **5-10 minutes** when you arrive at work, after lunch, and before leaving to look at your trigger lists. Take this time to do a **search pattern** of your workstation and **put away** non-essential items, such as work that needs to be filed, trash, and any other items that do not belong on your desk.

7. Keep a small phone book or roller deck for phone numbers, emails addresses, etc. on your desk.

8. If you can have a small bulletin board, place it near your workstation and tack up key memos or upcoming announcements that are part of your job. Remove old notes that are no longer relevant.

9. If you are moving about your workplace, try to keep a **small notepad** with you to jot down new information. It is easy to get distracted and lose focus of your trigger when someone stops you and gives out new tasks, or when a new idea pops into your mind. People with ADHD are more easily distracted and often forget information they receive orally. During the next 5-10-minute organizational interval, take out the notepad and log the new information, readjusting triggers and plans.

10. Starting a new job or task:

First, **define** the task. List all aspects of the job or task. Then prioritize the list in order of importance.

List the materials you will need.

Keep a list of **questions** that arise as you define your task.

Ask for **clarification**. Talk to others who have done this job before you, and see if a system already exists. There is no need to reinvent the wheel.

Consider **time** parameters. Try to estimate how much time each task may take. Give yourself extra time to adjust plans.

Go through a few **practice** trials. Re-evaluate and re-define steps. Remember to stay on the Experience Road, being positive and patient. If you become frustrated, step away and do a **Calm Out**. Taking five minutes to clear your head and relax your body will allow more oxygen to flow into your brain. With a clear head, you will find it easier to adjust to mistakes and find your path.

Updating this handout: Many people have now become comfortable with electronic devices such as phones, iPads, and computers to control the information flow. Many of these tasks can work well in these modalities. My handout is designed to teach organization and develop the ability to set triggers, plan, stay on task, and evaluate progress. For a considerable number of people, particularly those with ADHD, the electronic world can be very overwhelming to operationally understand. Use the paper and pencil methods to initially grasp the concepts, and incorporate electronics in small steps.

Updated August 2020

Figure 24

Inventory:
How is your business? Finding you

1. List 5 things you like about yourself. Does your partner know?
2. List 5 turn-ons. Does your partner know?
3. List 5 hobbies or interests. When have you last enjoyed them?
4. List 3 hobbies or interests you would like to try.
5. List 3 vacation ideas you would love to try.
6. My greatest belief about life is...
7. What 5 things don't you like about yourself? Does your partner know?
8. List 3 fears you have.
9. When was the last time you had a date with your partner?
10. If someone wrote a book about you, what would you call it?
11. Do you still have fantasies? Does your partner know?
12. What do you do to relax?
13. What angers you? Does your partner know?
14. How often do you make new friendships? What do like in people?
15. What is your new script? Short and long term goals?

References

Bradshaw, J. (1992). *Homecoming: Reclaiming and championing your inner child.* New York, NY: Bantam.

Feingold, B.F (1975). *Why your child is hyperactive.* New York, NY: Random House.

Hanh, T.N. (1975). *The miracle of mindfulness.* Boston, MA: Beacon Press.

Jacobson, E. (1938). *Progressive muscle relaxation.* Chicago, IL: University of Chicago Press.

Perle, R.L., Reinach, J, & Hefter, R. (1977). *Sweet pickles.* New York, NY: Holt, Rinehart, & Winston.

Rapp, D.J., & Bamberg, D.L. (1986). *The impossible child in school--at home: A guide for caring teachers and parents.* Buffalo, NY: Practical Allergy Research Foundation.

Sagal, P. (2016, July 2). *Not my job: how much does producer Norman Lear know about Learjets* [Radio broadcast]. NPR. https://www.npr.org/2016/07/02/484009777/not-my-job-how-much-does-producer-norman-lear-know-about-learjets

Waters, V. (1980). *Rational stories for children.* New York, NY: Institute of Rational Emotive Therapy.

Wolpe, J. (1969). *The practice of behavioral therapy.* New York, NY: Pergamon Press.

About the Author

Born to Holocaust survivors in Cincinnati, Ohio, and raised in New York City, Dr. Michael Simon's childhood was greatly affected by the pain and suffering his parents had encountered. When he was 13, his father died unexpectedly, hurtling him into a whirlwind of anger and depression. He barely made it into college. But in his second year at C.W. Post College, he discovered psychology and began to understand his emotions, how they were shaped, and how to manage them.

Overcoming those early setbacks, he graduated with high honors and went directly into his clinical psychology doctoral studies.

He received his doctorate in School, Community, Clinical Psychology from Hofstra University, where he specialized in Cognitive Behavioral Approaches to Treatment. He also holds certificates from the Institute of Rational Psychotherapy and from the Milton Errikson Institute. In addition, he is recognized as a Qualified Psychologist from the Association of State and Provisional Psychology Boards.

Dr. Simon is a member of both the American and Washington, D.C., Psychological Associations and is proud to have served a term as president of the Nassau County Psychological Association. He worked for New York State's office of Mental Retardation and Developmental Disabilities, is a former member of the New York Psychological Association, and was also employed by the Salvation Army within its programs for juvenile delinquency. His private practice began in 1976.

Along the way, he learned to accept that each of us is a work in progress, from our first day until our last, and this understanding has become a fundamental part of his teaching approach to psychotherapy. Dr. Simon believes that each of us needs to do our emotional work each and every day, continuing to learn from our experiences to stay focused on being an adult.

During his 43-year career as a clinical psychologist, Dr. Simon tried to employ those fundamental ideals in his activities outside of his practice, and continues to do so now as he keeps moving forward along the Experience Road to Life. He enjoys hiking and serves as a hike leader with numerous hiking clubs. He also enjoys photography, sports, and science fiction. Having recently relocated to the Washington, D.C., area, with his wife, Maria, he is excited to further explore the region's stunning natural areas and endless museums. He also has two sons and two grandsons.

He invites you to learn more about him, his work, and his adventures at his website, DrMichaelJSimonPsychologist.com, and his blog, Drmjsimon51.medium.com.

www.ingramcontent.com/pod-product-compliance
Lightning Source LLC
LaVergne TN
LVHW021714060526
838200LV00050B/2653